Praise for *If God Is the Answer, What Is the Question?*

'A really illuminating and accessible book, conversational, honest, personal, but also marked by formidable intellectual clarity. This is a most welcome addition to a new wave of innovative thinking about faith and philosophy.'

Rowan Williams

'Could any book be as good as the title of this one? Yes! Reading this book is like having a really interesting conversation with a wise, learned man, by turns dense and learned, by turns light and humorous. It addresses the deepest questions we could ever ask ourselves; it draws on a profound knowledge of the great philosophers, especially Kant; and it is warm and loving. I know that I shall often return to it.'

A. N. Wilson

'Philosophy and theology are not there to dispel the mysteries of life – even the frightening ones – but to lead us deeper into them. But for that, we need friends. This book is full of knowledge and love of philosophers and theologians of all stripes, and shares them generously. But above all, it befriends us, in our many fears and yearnings; and doing so, it gives us courage to figure out what our questions are.'

Judith Wolfe, author of *The Theological Imagination*

'Philosophy as it ought to be done: thoughtful, modest, many-sided, engaging, deeply learned and absolutely accessible. Christopher Insole won't try to tell you what to think or how to feel, about God or anything else, but reading this book will surely open up new ways of thinking about belief, unbelief and much besides. The fruits of decades of learning and thinking are offered here with a light touch, with humility, and with enormous generosity.'

Karen Kilby, author of *God, Evil and the Limits of Theology*

'Powerfully felt, personally engaged and lucidly presented, Insole's fascinating study uncovers surprisingly different ways of believing or disbelieving in God, and helps us understand what such belief or disbelief really amounts to.'

John Cottingham, author of *In Search of the Soul*

'Intelligent, compelling but above all compassionate, *If God Is the Answer, What Is the Question?* is a remarkable and necessary book for our troubled times. Writing with elegance, and wearing his erudition lightly, Insole offers a profound reconsideration of our connectedness to each other – and something we need even more: hope.'

Anna Beer, author of *Eve Bites Back*

'We have forgotten just how capacious the concept of God can be. Breaking free from the procrustean argumentative bed that is standard academic philosophy of religion, Insole invites readers into a space of curiosity and empathy. We wave at past and future selves, listen to stories of love and loss, and encounter understandings of God as diverse as the mysterious deep order and harmony of the world, the necessary totality of everything, and the transcendent reality of freedom and reason. God can be much more and quite other than a supernatural being. An irresistibly winsome volume.'

Jennifer A. Herdt, author of *Assuming Responsibility*

'This book is the clearest demonstration today of why philosophy matters. Surprisingly funny and deeply moving, *If God Is the Answer, What Is the Question?* is a book about God that is really about us: the different ways we get by, and how to see each other across those differences.'

Lexi Eikelboom, author of *Rhythm: A Theological Category*

'Drawing beautifully on an array of first-personal experiences, including his own, Christopher Insole develops a powerful vision of how we might converse about God, in ways that give due recognition to the rootedness of the language of God in the flow of life.'

Mark Wynn, author of *Spiritual Traditions and the Virtues: Living Between Heaven and Earth*

'At the heart of Insole's book is a story about faith. Not one that tells you what to believe or whom, if anyone, to believe in, but one that yearns to discover the horizons of the life we live together. Insole reminds us that if God is the answer, then the question is one we must each discover.'

Benjamin DeSpain, author of *Thinking Theologically about the Divine Ideas*

If God
Is the Answer,
What Is the
Question?

Christopher Insole

ONEWORLD

A Oneworld Book

First published by Oneworld Publications Ltd in 2026

Copyright © Christopher Insole, 2026

The moral right of Christopher J. Insole to be identified as the Author of this work has been asserted by him in accordance with the Copyright, Designs and Patents Act 1988

ISBN 978-1-83643-215-9
eISBN 978-1-83643-216-6

Typeset by Geethik Technologies
Printed and bound in Great Britain by Clays Ltd, Elcograf S.p.A.

The poems 'Friend with a Mandolin', 'Salterns' and 'At a Requiem Mass:
In Memory of Jim Insole' are the copyright of Jeremy Hooker.
Reproduced with the permission of Jeremy Hooker. Excerpt from the poem
'Walking Away' from *Complete Poems* by C. Day-Lewis reprinted by permission
of Peters Fraser & Dunlop on behalf of the Estate of C. Day-Lewis. 'Walking Away' from *Complete Poems*
by C. Day-Lewis published by Sinclair-Stevenson. Copyright © The Estate of
C. Day Lewis, 1992. Reprinted by permission of The Random House Group Limited.
Excerpt from the poem 'Water' from *The Whitsun Weddings* by Philip Larkin.
Reprinted by permission of Faber and Faber Ltd.
Excerpt from 'The Incarnate One' from *Collected Poems* by Edwin Muir.
Reprinted by permission of Faber and Faber Ltd.

The authorised representative in the EEA is eucomply OU,
Pärnu mnt 139b–14, 11317 Tallinn, Estonia
(email: hello@eucompliancepartner.com / phone: +33757690241)

Oneworld Publications Ltd
10 Bloomsbury Street
London WC1B 3SR
England

Stay up to date with the latest books,
special offers, and exclusive content from
Oneworld with our newsletter

Sign up on our website
oneworld.co.uk

MIX
Paper | Supporting
responsible forestry
FSC® C018072

This book is dedicated to the memory of James Insole (1940–2016) and Jeremy Hooker (1941–2025). To Jim and Jerry.

Contents

I

Arguing

What does arguing about God achieve?

In the autumn of 1996, there are two men arguing, in a room at the top of a staircase. One is a young man, the other is in mid-life.

They are disagreeing about what God would be like, if there were a God.

The older of the two thinks that God, if there is a God, should be construed as existing within time, as you and I do, albeit with more powers and insight. The younger man thinks that God should be construed as existing outside of time, as being present, somehow, to all times, a bit like, say, numbers, or mathematical truths.

They go at it for about an hour.

The older man wins the argument.

He always does.

They have argued before.

But the younger man does not shift his firmly held position one jot.

He never has, and never will.

Nonetheless, the next week, the two men agree to meet again and argue about something else, in relation to God.

Neither, ever, changes his mind, or persuades the other.

They could meet once a week for a hundred years, and nothing would ever change.

*

The older man, in mid-life, is Richard Swinburne, at the time the Nolloth professor of the philosophy of Christian religion at the University of Oxford. He is, without doubt, one of the most significant analytical philosophers of religion of the late twentieth century and early twenty-first century, providing rigorous arguments in favour of the existence of God.

The younger man is me, studying for a master's degree in philosophical theology. We are discussing my 'assignment', an essay on the topic of God and time.

After the master's degree, I went on to do a doctorate, and then became a university lecturer, and then a professor. For twenty-five years I have written my own arguments, often in relation to the idea of God, and taught others how to argue, according to certain canons and protocols.

I am now about the same age as Richard Swinburne would have been in 1996.

I am a bit perplexed at why it has taken me so long to be perplexed at the failure of such arguments to change minds.

Think about the energy and precision that goes into constructing, and critiquing, philosophical proofs for the existence of God, or for other core religious commitments. At the same time, consider how common it is to observe that no one (or very few people) ever has been, or will be, persuaded one way or another on these matters by a philosophical argument.

The asymmetry between the effort and the likely success of the effort is remarkable.

The book is driven by two simple questions.

What might be going on – *really* going on – when some people are drawn to talking about *God*, others are repelled by it, and others are indifferent? How might we have better conversations about the full range of what is really going on?

What do I mean by 'going on' in the first question? Well, we would expect it to include explicit rational arguments and convictions, certainly, but also formative experiences, feeling and desire. The answer might help us answer the second question, and find a better way to talk about these and the relationship between, say, abstract thinking, arguments, formative experiences and emotion.

What this book tries to do, in relation to the God question, is to think about:

> What is really going on, for and between you and
> me?

*

There are a number of ways in which we might approach this task.

One approach might be sociological and anthropological: to study, as best we can, what sort of causes or conditions bring about religious or non-religious people, and then, how such groups of people express these commitments in different contexts. Or, we might take a more statistical and data-driven psychological approach: what percentage of a population, living under such-and-such conditions, self-identify as or behave in ways that can be considered religious?

All these approaches are valuable and have their place. I draw on some anthropological studies in the course of this book, when they help to address some of our questions. But what we notice is that such approaches, however intriguing and informative, may not really address the second part of the question:

> What is really going on, *for and between you and me*?

I find out, let us say, that thirty percent of people living in such-and-such conditions self-identify as atheists. Or, I learn about the beliefs and practices of self-identifying pagans in England in the 1980s, or self-identifying humanists in 2011. Fine, and good: but what about me and you? How are we involved and drawn in, if we are neither witches in the 1980s, nor humanists in 2011? If I read a sociological study, and then wonder how it applies to me – 'which group do I belong to?' – I am regarding myself in the third person, observing myself as an object of study. But we understand ourselves best from the inside – not when trying to observe ourselves, but when living out the moments that most define us. It is when alone in the small hours of the night, or when joyously unfurling in conversation with a beloved, or when fearing, perhaps, that we might die soon, or that we would like to die, or when dearly hoping to live, here, now, with this person, doing meaningful work, raising a child, building a life together.

At these points you and I are inside of ourselves, looking out at the world, wondering what our place in it might be, or might become.

When we face such moments, how do we achieve greater self-knowledge, or knowledge, compassion and empathy for each other? How do we have better conversations or disagreements? What sort of enquiry will help us, you and me, to do *this*?

*

What is the discipline that you turn to, when you can't know stuff, when the facts run out?

A scene in the film *Indiana Jones and the Last Crusade* has the hero, played by Harrison Ford, lecturing to a group of university students. He writes the word 'FACT' on the board, and announces that archaeology is about facts, not truth, or the meaning of life. Professor Jones tells the class that if they want to think about the meaning of life, Dr Tyree's philosophy class is further along the corridor.

The discipline you turn to when the facts run out is philosophy.

Let's take up Professor Jones's suggestion and go down the hall.

Part of what philosophy does is search for self-knowledge, to understand what is really going on, and in a way that involves you and me, possibly offering consolation, challenge, transformation, healing, empathy, encouragement. Philosophy can, and has to, draw on a wide range of evidence and types of evidence to help in this search. If it is to be self-involving, to give us some 'yes!' moments of recognition, we will need more than just observations and statistics. We will need to see other thinkers lay out their worldviews, to think about, and to feel, where and why we do or do not share these views. We will need texts from philosophers and theologians, from atheists and believers. Some of these texts will offer us arguments, but some of them will be more about experience, emotion, individual narratives, fundamental dispositions, the unconscious, childhood formation.

All of this will be helpful and needed to uncover what is really going on, for and between you and me. We can even draw on, and should draw on, our own experiences and emotions, where and when that is a type of evidence, relevant to the question at hand.

The point is not to try to get to know more about God, or about whether or not God exists – not directly anyway. It is to understand ourselves and each other better, and to revere and honour, and learn from, the different ways we get through, and get by. The goal is simple and humble: to foster more intellectual compassion towards, and between, different types of believer and non-believer. If you want to understand belief, or lack of it, you must attend to the believer, or the non-believer, in all their vulnerability and sincerity, doing their best to get by, in all the hours, days and months that are framed by the different ways of not being here: being not yet born, and having passed away.

2

Yearning

What is the question to which God might be the answer?

I came out religious, it seems.

That is to say, I do not remember a time when I did not believe in God, although I was not brought up in a religious or churched household.

Believing in God seemed as natural as breathing.

In later childhood and early teenage years, if I had had to formulate an 'argument' for belief in God, the answer would have been something like the following:

I believe in God because of the problem of evil.

This isn't quite how the problem of evil is supposed to work, or the way it is typically presented.

Usually the existence of so much evil and suffering is given as one of the main reasons not to believe in God. If God is perfectly good, all-knowing and all-powerful, why does God not prevent terrible evil and suffering?

But it seemed to me obvious that the existence of evil and suffering was the best sort of reason to believe in God, as an expression of a type of yearning. God was the concept that should be reached for on the other side of a lament. No other concept would suffice, because it would be inadequate to the task of engaging with evil. Anything else would be unrealistic: no amount of historical or political action, or human self-improvement, or economic management, or whatever, could possibly address the evil and suffering that had already happened, let alone prevent or ameliorate what was to come.

In other words: the problem in the problem of evil is not God, I thought, but evil. Evil is the problem, to which God is the answer.

I think I probably tried to express this thought in school, and soon learned that it was not one of the grooves down which one's mind was supposed to travel. At least, the formal problem went the other way round: the existence of evil and suffering is a problem for belief in God, not a good motivation for it. I learned to keep (mostly) quiet about this. Until now.

*

At a certain age, the problem of evil would have been my attempted answer to the framing question of this chapter:

> What is the problem, to which God might be the
> answer?

If we step out a bit, we might be able to identify a more fundamental problem, of which the problem of evil is just one manifestation. The more fundamental problem might be not feeling quite at home in the world, or universe, whilst very much wanting to.

If you don't care much about 'feeling at home in the universe', there won't be a problem here.

You might respond that it is enough to feel at home *at home*, in a more low-key way. In which case 'feeling at home in the universe' won't be a problem to which God might be an answer. There may be no problem to which God could be an answer. That's fine.

To feel the tug towards the concept of God, you may have to begin by not feeling at home in the world, and *wanting very much, sometimes, to do so*. There has to be an element of *yearning*.

The form that this yearning takes can vary, depending on where one feels the fault lines, the problems, to be. I've already set out one possible version of the yearning, one facet of wanting to feel at home in the world: the desire to address the problem of evil and suffering. I will give three more examples, which many people feel at different times, and which have been of concern to some philosophers. These examples will be the following:

A yearning for significance, given the problem of the vastness of the universe.

A yearning for freedom, given the way in which we may feel determined by our genetics or by the weight of historical and political forces.

A yearning for a type of harmony and unity in our relationships with human beings and with non-human nature, given all the clashes and fractures in perspective that we encounter.

*

Before saying something about each of these, I want to address a question that might arise here:

Why all this variety?

You thought, perhaps, that you were going to be presented with a single answer or theory to the question: 'What is the problem, to which God might be the answer?'

Well, in a way, I have offered a single platform to think about a variety of answers: the yearning to be at home in the world. But the variety is important, and will run through the book. In 1902 the philosopher and psychologist William James wrote a book called *The Varieties of Religious Experience: a Study in Human Nature.*[1] James addresses the issue of the great variety of types of religious experience and commitment.

James asks the following:

> [I]s the existence of so many religious types and
> sects and creeds regrettable?

I would want to expand the terms of this question to include 'types' who do not believe in God at all, or who are opposed to belief in God. The answer that James gives seems, to me, to be the correct one, and, in different ways, I'll be making this case throughout the book:

> I answer 'No' emphatically.[2]

When we think about it, and consider the people we know and cherish, as well as the people we find intolerable, isn't this sort of obvious? Although, as with many things, it can be forgotten in the heat of arguing for something we deeply care about.

*

When thinking about God, I think it is simply not possible to hope for knowledge, or certainty, or even high probability. Nor, I would submit, will knowledge or certainty ever be possible.

Think of all the time, over all the centuries, and the failure to arrive at agreement or certainty: all the disputation and disagreement, some of it peaceful and intellectual, some of it violent and primitive.

Think of your own case: how amenable are *you*, really, to a powerful argument or piece of evidence unsettling and changing your own belief or non-belief, or your long-held agnosticism?

Some people, however, think there is a demonstrably correct answer and they know what it is. If you want something more in this line, other books are available. They have give-away titles such as *Is There a God?* (the answer in that book is 'yes'), *There is a God* (an even more emphatic 'yes'), and *The God Delusion* (a big 'no' this time). If you yourself already *know*, you may still enjoy this book as an insight into what seems to be troubling others.

Reason and investigation are limited in this area because of the unknowability of what people reach out to, when they embrace, or reject, the idea of God and the divine.

Reason and investigation do not have similar limits, thank goodness, in other areas, such as vaccine research. In the area of vaccine research, talking about our emotions, and consulting our feelings, would be a bad idea. Please follow the evidence. Only consider emotion insofar as you need to control for it – to eliminate 'confirmation bias', for example – and prevent it from distorting your evaluation of the evidence. Other areas are more nuanced, and share some of the limitations of thinking and talking about

God, including ethics ('what is morally required of me and you?'), aesthetics ('what is beauty?'), or politics ('how do we live alongside one another?'). I don't need to take a line on these issues here; we've enough on our plates thinking about God.

So, when thinking and talking about God, what are we going to do next?

One answer – fairly popular in some circles – is to say that we should all stop believing in God, precisely because of the variety. The impossibility of arriving at knowledge or certainty *proves* that there is no God.

I've several thoughts about this.

First of all, it simply isn't very realistic, is it? Just to insist that everyone stop believing in God.

An entirely unrealistic proposal isn't really very rational, in the end. We know this from the historical record: every attempt to change people's beliefs about God, from Robespierre's Cult of the Supreme Being to the multiple Soviet campaigns against religion, have required force, and have failed miserably.

It is worth thinking about why it is unrealistic to ask that people just 'stop believing' in God. In part, it is the difficulty of controlling the beliefs and feelings of other people. But, more fundamentally, the problem is that people can't easily control their *own* beliefs and feelings. Belief and unbelief are too thickly woven into our whole sense of self, and our way of being in the world. Given this, other approaches may be necessary – such as, for example, the approach I'm taking here, of exploring, in a broad and deep sense, 'what is really going on?'

Secondly, the claim that variety and lack of certainty *prove* that there is no God is a claim to a type of knowledge and certainty, about the non-existence of God. As I say, I don't think certainty or knowledge can be achieved on either side of this debate.

It is an interesting philosophical claim. We could describe it as a sort of theorem:

> Where there is variety of beliefs about *x*, *x* is all
> bollocks.

This is not, though, a true claim. You can see this if you insert different values for *x*: moral truth, political virtue, black holes. But it is an interesting claim – and not self-evidently false either – and I will return to different aspects of this 'variety = bollocks' thesis at relevant points.

Thirdly, belief and unbelief in God are of such wide interest and importance to so many people. Almost everyone has some idea of their position on the question. And almost everyone finds it particularly irritating to have someone try to convert them from one of these positions to another. It almost always feels like an insult and an imposition. This is interesting also, and points to the feature I commented on above: that belief or unbelief is so woven into our sense of self, and our way of being in the world. If you try to convert me, you are saying: the way you are in the world is not fine. You need re-engineering. In response, our reaction might be: yes, but are *you* – you ideological nutcase – really the one to do this to me?

One further observation is that even amongst the groups that identify with unbelief and agnosticism, there is a widespread desire, often, to reach out for 'something' beyond, something a bit transcendent, a something, we know not what. This drive for a 'something else' is part of the human condition, which we all suffer from, more or less. One might think here of the French philosopher Blaise Pascal, who speaks of a type of memory of 'true happiness' in every human heart, 'of which there now remain…only the mark and empty trace'. We try 'in vain' to 'fill' this void, 'seeking from things absent' the help we do not 'obtain in things present'. All such efforts are inadequate, as 'the infinite abyss can only be filled…by God'.[3] And, if there is no God, the void may remain, and, perhaps, for some, that is how it must be.

The more familiar, and not inaccurate, paraphrase of Pascal's thought here is:

> There is a God-shaped hole in the heart of each man which cannot be satisfied by any created thing.

Or, as St Augustine put it, speaking directly to God:

> Our hearts are restless, till they rest in Thee.[4]

So, again, given all this: what are we going to do?

Probably not try to convert each other, one way or another.

We could try, instead, continuing to talk about the varieties of ways in which some people don't feel quite at home in the cosmos.

*

One variety of not feeling at home in the cosmos arises from the problem of evil and suffering.

A second variety I want to discuss arises from a giddy sense of the vastness of the universe, and the conviction of our own insignificance which this can bring.

If you are asked to 'think about your life', you might bring to mind everything that is most important to you: your hopes and plans, the people you love, and the things in the world you would most like to do something about. These things will seem like they *really matter*; and they do, because you, as a human being, are important. But, if you have ever tried thinking about the vastness of space, or of time, you might suddenly feel very small and insignificant: think of all the hundreds of millions of years the earth existed without any sort of life, or all the billions of galaxies.

The two ways of looking at yourself do not fit together very easily. In the first, you are the centre of a world; in the second, you are a tiny speck.

The contemporary philosopher Thomas Nagel writes about this clash of perspectives. We exert effort and strain, to feed and clothe ourselves, to maintain our health and appearance, to engage in meaningful life projects, and to be, for example, an adequate parent, spouse, friend and colleague. We strive, and persevere, sometimes flourishing, and, at other times, suffering. At the same time, we are able to see, indeed, we are unable to avoid seeing ourselves, the whole sorry struggle, from a more bracing and detached point of view:

> Humans have the special capacity to step back and survey themselves, and the lives to which they are committed, with that detached amazement which comes from watching an ant struggle up a heap of sand.[5]

We are able to regard ourselves, and all the effort, as if we were not ourselves. And it looks 'at once sobering and comical'.[6]

Where might God come in? Well, if you think that there is something in the universe, or beyond it, that offers the hope that these two ways of looking can come together and achieve an ultimate harmony and unity: perhaps, this is what is pointed to by the word 'God', or 'the divine'. The coming together might not be possible yet, in this life. Or, it might be something achieved in our own mind, through spiritual practices and meditation.

Maybe, sometimes, for some people, God might be the answer to the problem of the vastness of the universe, against our own apparent insignificance.

Knowing what sort of thing the word 'God' does in our language is not the same as knowing exactly what, or who, God is. At least, though, we might have a better idea of what we are looking for, whether or not we think we find it. We might note, though, that any God who addresses this vastness problem is unlikely to be an old bearded man sitting on a cloud. Such a genial fellow would likely have the same perplexing questions about his own existence as we do. This bearded gentleman might be drawn to belief in God as well, and so could hardly be God himself.

*

In addition to the opposing perspectives we can take of ourselves, there is the problem of everyone else's perspectives upon us, and the perspectives we adopt in relation to those others. So much of the pain and joy of life is made up of this: discovering ourselves in a friendship, losing ourselves in a romance, growing into parenthood, grieving at a sense of alienation from a friend, meaning something to a pupil, mentor or teacher, speaking at an event, and in so doing, 'representing' something to those present. All the roles and masks we put on, and those we find ourselves already wearing, make up an enormous part of our being in the world. It manifests in the clothes we choose, the way we style our hair (or lack thereof), the food we buy, the holidays we take, the books we read, the people we befriend, the jobs and hobbies we reach for. Some roles we may enjoy, others we might try to escape or recast. Some, we simply have to live with. How much of ourselves is lost, squashed or maimed in this process? And how much vitality do we gain, or lose, from the roles we play in the lives of others?

At times, we might agree with Jean-Paul Sartre: 'Hell is other people.'

But what if, somehow, all these perspectives could all come together, beautifully, dancingly, harmoniously?

The English poet and essayist Jeremy Hooker is not traditionally religious. 'Agnostic', 'pantheist', 'animist' and 'sceptical' are words he has used to describe himself. Nonetheless, Hooker reflects that the word 'God' might stand for a 'need that makes an idea possible', which is 'the need to think that, though we cannot fully know ourselves, there is a perspective in which we are fully known'.[7] Hooker is naming the fragments that make up our lives, where 'complete self-knowledge and complete knowledge of another person are equal impossibilities':

> With our mixed motives, with the knot of contradictions that we are, and with the relationships that make us, as beings subject to change, who live in time, there is no position from which we can gain complete self-knowledge. We are always on the inside of our own faces, and in life, so that ideas of the self tend to be waxwork ideas, perceptions of ourselves as effigies.[8]

The idea of God, for Hooker, circles around, as he puts it, 'a need that makes the idea possible': the need for all possible perspectives being seen at once, in a way that tessellates, harmonises, integrates and, revealing all, forgives all.

The contemporary philosophical theologian Judith Wolfe writes about this idea, from a more committed theological perspective. Wolfe acknowledges the importance of 'telling our story', the narrative of our lives, but reflects:

> [T]he more we insist on our individual stories, the less aware we often are how conventional the roles we take are, how influenced by the narrative

models peddled by the latest films, books, or influencers. What feels like authenticity is often mere cliché.[9]

When lost in cliché (the perfect lover, mother, father, brother, man, woman), we can become 'rigid', in a way that forces 'other people into roles within our narrative, selecting and matching their actions to a pattern that makes sense within the plot unfolding in *our* mind':

> We are always the *protagonists* of our own lives, and cast others in roles vis-à-vis ourselves with which they (almost by definition) cannot themselves fully identify: supporting roles, or antagonistic ones. Of course we acknowledge, at least in theory, that others, too, are protagonists to themselves; but it is something of which we need continually to remind ourselves. Conversely, what role we play in one another's consciousness is very little under our control.

This can lead, Wolfe suggests, to 'profound loneliness and disorientation'. We become 'to each other not real persons in a shared space, whose relative movements *affect* one another, but apparitions slotted into plays or stories that are increasingly of one's solitary imagining':

The more we insist on the role of protagonist and cast others into supporting or antagonistic roles, the more we manoeuvre ourselves into competition or worse, find ourselves the only players among non-player characters in a cosmos without coordinates.[10]

If this is the problem – the split and fragmented roles we play, in our own lives and the lives of others – in what sense is God the answer?

Wolfe unfurls the following response:

To some extent, the simple answer is that theology believes that we are not the ultimate tellers of the stories of our lives; that our lives are, indeed, part of a larger story, in which we do not have to be perfect protagonists, but are, as sinners loved by God, forgiven and restored to a story in which love places *all* at the centre and *all* at the service of others.[11]

Wolfe draws on the story of Orual from C. S. Lewis's *Till we Have Faces*. The story Orual 'tells about herself crumbles in her hands and runs through her fingers':

[I]t is only when she hears her own story narrated by a god that she, too, can be Psyche, *soul*; that her story turns out to be intertwined, redemptively, with the stories of those she loves but has wounded and lost.

Wolfe reflects, 'this may well be the form that the last judgement will take: this re-telling of our stories that integrates them into a larger story of love':

It is our fervent hope that this will be so.[12]

3

Stupid

Do you have to be stupid or infantile to believe in God?

If you were walking the streets of any large UK city in the year 2008, you might have seen the following slogan on the side of a bus:

> There's probably no god. Now stop worrying and enjoy your life.[1]

This is the 'Atheist bus campaign', sponsored by the British Humanist Association (BHA), as it was then known. Since 2008 it has changed its name to 'Humanists UK'.

The most interesting premise of the slogan, for me, is not the assumption that there is 'probably' no God (although they mean 'definitely'). Far more interesting is the assumption that realising this will help us to stop worrying, and will enhance our ability to enjoy ourselves.

The anthropologist Matthew Engelke carried out a study on BHA meetings and literature.[2] He found that being happy, and being happy now, is a particularly high priority for humanists.

Engelke draws attention to the logo for the humanist movement, which was selected, in 1965, out of 150 entries in a competition: the 'happy human'. It features in the lapel pins of some BHA members, which read 'Happy Humanist' or 'Good without God'.[3] Engelke considers a project put together by the humanist Andrew West, 'a series of portraits of humanists accompanied by their answers to the question':

What are you happy about?[4]

Each entry begins: 'I am happy today because'. Following this tag is a wide list of entries: including 'children', 'food, drink, flowers', 'birds', 'consumption', 'television shows, clothes, a new pair of stilettos – even the purchase of a camper van'.[5]

The celebration of 'happiness' and the 'here and now' is contrasted with approaches that, it is thought, do not lead to happiness, or locate happiness in the beyond, in the supernatural. A negative reference to religion is part and parcel of this commitment to happiness. As Engelke puts it, 'it is the language of the Enlightenment that dominates':

[O]ne particular version of the Enlightenment story has pride of place: that in which reason snuffs out religion and gives rise to a modern world governed by science.[6]

The happiness of the humanist is also an implied critique of religion. When the humanist proclaims that 'she loves her new heels', this is not 'at core to betray her entrapment by the "treadmill" of consumption. Or, at least, it is not only ever that':

> For what such embracement of earthly pleasures is also supposed to suggest is that there are only earthly pleasures to be had – that we are each our own makers. Humanists use their stilettos to beat God over the head; they use their camper vans to run him down the road. They use their chances to explain why they're happy to be happy here and now in a way that underscores its ethical valences.[7]

It is all 'about being good without God'.[8]

Why be so down on God?

And what does being so down on God have to do with the emphasis on being happy, and being good?

Certainly, believing in God can make some people unhappy, if they are riven with guilt or shame, or have a persecutory vision of the Almighty; and some people can do terrible things in the name of religion.

But what about all the happy and good people who be-lieve in God? The kind people, who flourish and cherish others?

Maybe God is a delusion.

But what if it is a delusion that helps me to worry less? What if I enjoy life more with this delusion?

It is at this point that we get to the rub, and to the open-ing question of this chapter:

> Do you have to be stupid, or infantile, to believe
> in God?

It is clear that some humanists are convinced that you *do* have to be stupid or infantile to believe in God. You might not be stupid and infantile overall, but with respect to this belief, stupid and/or infantile is what you are.

Being stupid and infantile isn't good, and if it does make you happy, it really shouldn't.

Grow up, and get your kicks elsewhere.

*

At the time of Engelke's research (2011), the BHA could boast twelve thousand members paying an annual fee of £35, and a further eighteen thousand supporters who re-ceived updates of BHA events and meetings.[9] Amongst high-profile members of the BHA, Engelke lists Richard

Dawkins and Stephen Fry, celebrity scientists Jim Al-Khalili, Brian Cox and Alice Roberts, the journalist Polly Toynbee, the philosopher A. C. Grayling, and novelists such as Philip Pullman and the late Terry Pratchett. Amongst supporters is the actor and comedian Ricky Gervais, about whom more in a bit. More broadly, Engelke reports that the demographic of the BHA is largely 'white', 'male', and 'well-educated':

> Just shy of 89 percent of members are 'White British'…just over 69 percent are male, and 72 percent of members have a university degree; 13 percent of these degrees are from Oxbridge.[10]

Of this number, twenty-four percent are 'members of a political party', and eighty percent 'donate at least monthly to one or more charities', 'giving some indication that this is a demographic with high levels of civic engagement'.[11]

The group identified by Engelke for study is, it must be said, a relatively small segment of the population, and a strikingly non-diverse one at that. Nonetheless, the humanist movement has a public intellectual profile in the UK that far outstrips the size of its official membership.

So, are the humanists correct? Do you have to be stupid, or infantile, to believe in God?

Or, as the lame and tattered fridge magnets in workplace common rooms might put it:

> You don't have to be stupid and infantile to be-
> lieve here, but it helps.

*

Let's take a look at the work of one of the most savage and high-profile public atheists, Richard Dawkins.

Amongst other things, we can find in Dawkins two assumptions about religion and belief in God:

(i) Belief in God is supposed to function as an explanation for why things are the way they are, or as a source of information about how the world is.

(ii) Belief in God, and using God language, involves believing in supernatural beings beyond the realm of nature.

On both counts, belief in God comes out as stupid and/or infantile: it is science that offers explanations for why things are as they are. Religion, belief in God or gods, is aligned with 'supernatural spells and stage tricks', which seem 'cheap and tawdry'[12] when compared with 'the facts of the real world as understood through the methods of science'.[13]

There are areas of life where we do not yet know the explanation, but if an explanation is ever to be had, it will be science that gets us there:

There is much that remains deeply mysterious, and it is not likely that we will ever uncover all the secrets of a universe as vast as ours: but, armed with science, we can at least ask sensible, meaningful questions about it and recognize credible answers when we find them. We don't have to invent wildly implausible stories: we have the joy and excitement of real scientific investigation and discovery to keep our imaginations in line. And in the end that is more exciting than fantasy.[14]

Furthermore, science shows us that there is no need to believe in supernatural beings, and no evidence for their existence. A type of fierce scorn for belief in God is never far from the surface in Dawkins's writing:

The whole world is made of incredibly tiny things, much too small to be visible to the naked eye – and yet none of the myths or so-called holy books that some people, even now, think were given to us by an all-knowing god, mentions them at all! In fact, when you look at those myths and stories, you can see that they don't contain any of the knowledge that science has patiently worked out. They don't tell us how big or how old the universe is: they don't tell us how to treat cancer; they don't explain gravity or the internal combustion engine; they don't tell

> us about germs, or nuclear fusion, or electricity,
> or anaesthetics. In fact, unsurprisingly, the stories
> in holy books don't contain any more information
> about the world than was known to the primitive
> peoples who first started telling them! If these 'holy
> books' really were written, or dictated, or inspired,
> by all-knowing gods, don't you think it's odd that
> those gods said nothing about any of these impor-
> tant and useful things?[15]

How infantile and stupid it is to believe, when one considers
that physics and chemistry are entirely absent from the Bible
and other holy books!

*

Einstein is generally thought to have been quite clever, and
pretty good at science. Here are some words from Einstein
about God and science:

> I'm not an atheist.
> Cosmic religious feeling [reveals] the futility of human de-
> sires and the sublimity and marvelous order which reveals
> itself both in nature and in the world of thought.
> Speaking of the spirit that informs modern scientif-
> ic investigations, I am of the opinion that all the finer

speculations in the realm of science spring from a deep religious feeling, and that without such feeling they would
not be fruitful.

I am a deeply religious man.

I believe in Spinoza's God who reveals himself in the orderly harmony of what exists.[16]

Now, of course, people who are clever about some things can
be stupid on others. And, wheeling out Einstein to trump
Dawkins may be entertaining – type B fun, admittedly –
but it is not actually an argument.

But it is an example of a widely shared feature of some
of the varieties of religious belief, of which Dawkins seems
oblivious. It concerns not so much 'whether God exists', but
how the word is being used. The word 'God', for Einstein,
is not the *explanation* for the laws of physics or the mysteries of the universe. Rather, it is the word that Einstein
reaches for to *describe and evoke* these laws and mysteries. I
will go on in the book to show that Einstein is by no means
alone here.

For Einstein, it is the lawfulness of the universe that is
divine. I'll be saying more about this, and what Einstein
might mean by 'Spinoza's God', in chapter 6. But, for
our purposes here, this is enough: the word God is not
being used as a further explanation, or as a source of
new facts. God *is* the mysterious and deep order and

harmony of what exists. Another way of putting this is to ask:

> What might we call the mysterious and deep order and harmony of what exists?

Einstein calls it God.

God is not the cause of the order and harmony. God didn't design it. God *is* it.

God is the word for the beauty and mystery of that which we cannot fully explain. 'God' is the word that Einstein wants to use.

I find this interesting.

So, we have a better question in front of us. Dawkins does not use the word God to describe or evoke these mysteries, and the beauty of reality. Einstein does. Which brings us to the opening question of the book.

> What is really going on?

What is at stake here? Why does one use the word God, and the other reject it?

Who is more stupid and infantile: Dawkins or Einstein?

This question is not going to give us the answer. It is not that the more stupid of the two will use the word God, because that is the stupid thing to do.

*

There are more refined versions of the hostility to God language, in philosophers who take more nuanced positions. I have noticed that when a philosopher worries that his or her position might be getting a bit 'spooky', a bit too close to something that looks religious, there can be a hasty signalling:

> I'm not doing that!

To prove this point, almost as if distancing oneself from the bullied kid, references to God or the divine are denigrated variously as being from the 'middle ages' or the 'dark ages', as being 'superstitious' or 'prescientific', as involving 'medieval superstition',[17] 'rampant Platonism',[18] or an 'injection of the supernatural', and as representing a recourse to pre-enlightenment animism or 'meta persons'. Consider, for example, Nagel's admission: not only does he not believe in a God, but, he admits, 'I hope there is not a God!':

> I don't want there to be a God; I don't want the universe to be like that.[19]

These are all examples from philosophers who are relatively sympathetic to religion, sometimes.

At the same time, there is (in some cases) an acknowledged unease about this quick dismissal of the category of divinity. Nagel himself admits to being 'strongly subject to' a culturally widespread 'fear of religion'. Nonetheless, Nagel considers that this same fear has 'large and often pernicious consequences for modern intellectual life', preventing some promising lines of thought, creativity and enquiry.[20]

Sometimes anecdote and personal experience can be a valid piece of evidence. Here we have Dawkins and others telling us what is going on when people embrace religious beliefs: they are looking for explanations for things, by making resort to supernatural beings.

I'm religious. As I said, I came out that way.

Many of my colleagues and students in different theology and religion departments are religious: not all of them, and perhaps not the majority, but quite a few of them. Probably a higher proportion than in most other academic departments, but perhaps not a higher proportion than in the general population. So, also, many (not all) of my friends and family believe in God, in some way, or did when they were alive. Depending on how things really are, some of the dead ones might still believe in God. If they are in a position to believe in anything at all, the probability that they believe in God will be quite high, I suspect. Maybe, it is better to say, they don't *believe* anymore. They know.

Or they don't. Because there is nothing, and they are nowhere. Gone, entirely, as once they were not yet.

Belief won't be coming into it at all.

Because religion and God is the sort of thing I like to talk about, I've spoken, or did speak, to most of these friends and colleagues about God, at some point.

I can honestly say that there is not *one* person I know for whom a search for an explanation of the origins or nature of the universe is the most significant motivation for belief in God. These lie more in the types of problems I set out in the last chapter: how to get through suffering and pain, how to think about our significance given the vastness and indifference of the universe, or how to think about freedom, or the clash of so many perspectives upon ourselves. My anecdotal experience is confirmed by a recently burgeoning literature exploring the psychological causes for belief in God.[21] A recent summary of these findings lists five prominent causes for belief in God: a need for control, a need to cope with death, suffering, a need for justice, and experiential thinking (roughly speaking, more intuitive and lateral thinking styles).[22] This seems about right to me, from my own personal experience, and the concept of 'yearning', although not employed in these studies, seems about right also.

Of course, this does not mean that belief in God is therefore justified or warranted, but it does indicate that God is not functioning simply or mainly as an *explanation* or a theory. God is a sort of gathering concept for where a mystery meets a search for intelligibility, or for hope, or for peace.

Now, *some* of the people who I know do accept the following pattern of thinking: given that we have other grounds or motivations for belief in God, this belief may offer some sort of explanation for some features of the world we live in. But these features never 'rival' science, or act as an alternative source of information. If anything, they help to explain why science is able to be so successful: 'why is there so much order and harmony that is amenable to scientific investigation?'

Why is this relevant?

Well, the suggestion is that belief in God is infantile or stupid, because it involves crass explanations invoking supernatural beings. This can only be true if belief in God involves looking for an explanation – crass or otherwise – and if it involves invoking supernatural beings.

And this just isn't true: this isn't what most people are *actually* doing when they believe in God.

So, whatever the stupidity is, this is not it, and this, typically, *is* the stupidity that is pointed at in the humanist critique.

There is an irony about all this. Dawkins has no formal training in philosophy, but is one of the most influential pedlars of a philosophical position in the wider culture in the last few decades. Dawkins is, though, trained in the empirical method, and understands the importance of going out and observing what is happening in the world, rather than making it up according to his prejudices and desires.

My respectful, if barbed, request to Dawkins, and to others, is that more empirical observation and curiosity in this area would be welcome. Play to your strengths, and to your training. And, maybe, approach the philosophy with a little more humility and openness.

*

Why does the accusation that religious people are infantile or stupid have such traction?

I suspect that there are a lot of causes and reasons, and some of them involve quite a lot of emotion and unconscious factors.

But at the more argumentative and conscious end of things, I do have an idea about what has been going on, especially in 'academic' circles. I'd like to come at this through an anecdote, relayed by an influential twentieth-century philosopher called Bernard Williams.[23]

Williams describes a group of Oxford philosophers in the early part of the twentieth century preparing translations of Aristotle. One philosopher insists on translating a Greek term, entirely anachronistically, as 'moral obligation', and then proceeds to write articles, and build a career, complaining about Aristotle's 'inadequate theory of moral obligation'.

Just so, I think, we have accepted, or promulgated, or suffered from, inadequate translations of the concept of God: 'God is this', it is said, where what is pointed out ranges from a childish wish-fulfilment fantasy, to an interventionist busybody, to a crude anthropomorphism (the Nobodaddy in the sky).

And then, obviously enough, the reaction will be:

> I do not see how anyone could believe in this God.

Dawkins constantly complains about the belief in supernatural beings, or a supernatural being. But look, again, at Einstein. When Einstein talks about God, he is not referring to anything supernatural at all. It is his word for the deep mystery of the *natural*.

Later on in the book, I will also reflect on theological positions that are committed to something 'beyond' the universe, which is called God, and which is conceived of in 'personal' terms. But, even here, the 'personal' God is not a person like you or me, and is not captured by the crude critique that religious believers have, as it were, an invisible friend, a bit like you and me, but nicer and more powerful.

I'm eager to reinforce the sense that there is a great variety of ways in which the concept of God, or the divine, has been used, even within the fairly narrow constraints of 'Western' philosophy.

I want to show you some of this variety, and to celebrate it.

As we've seen, one of the complaints of Dawkins and other humanist atheists is precisely the variety. Consider this

dialogue from the bleak, but tender and humane, comedy
After Life, in which Gervais stars. Tony, played by Gervais,
is in deep mourning for his wife, who has recently died of
cancer. His 'superpower', he explains, is that he 'doesn't give
a fuck anymore'. He can say what he wants, whenever he
wants, to anyone, and, if it all gets too much, he can kill
himself. Several times in the series he does try to kill himself. It is his dog that keeps him alive: demanding a walk or
some food, or, simply, loving him, at the abysmal moment
of choice, when holding the tablets, or when walking fully
clothed into the sea.

In one scene, Tony turns to his office co-worker Kath,
played by Diane Morgan, who insists that she believes in
God, and asks Tony: 'How can you not believe?'

Tony:	Which one?
Kath:	What do you mean?
Tony:	Well…er, Zeus?
Kath:	Who?
Tony:	Greek God. Or Ra, or Ganesh?
Kath:	No, not those ones, the real one in the Bible.
Tony:	Yahweh.
Kath:	Just God.
Tony:	Well, you know how you don't believe in all those other gods I mentioned. That's how I don't believe in yours.

This is, I know, a standard humanist/atheist line of attack, akin to a well-rehearsed move in mixed martial arts. It is a dramatised version of the 'variety = bollocks' theorem we have explored.

You might remember that when William James asked, 'Is the existence of so many religious types and sects and creeds regrettable?' He answered in the negative. Here's what he has to say about why:

> My reason is that I do not see how it is possible that creatures in such different positions and with such different powers as human individuals are, should have exactly the same functions and the same duties. No two of us have identical difficulties, nor should we be expected to work out identical solutions. Each, from his peculiar angle of observation, takes in a certain sphere of fact and trouble, which each must deal with in a unique manner.[24]

To make this stand as a response to Tony/Gervais, more would need to be said. And it will be. But at this point, we might just say: believing in God is not stupid. Einstein is not stupid. Also, *not* believing in God is not stupid. Dawkins is not stupid.

Dawkins can be, at times, sarcastic and dismissive. But, for all I know, this may come from a place of pain. Dawkins is popular and influential for a reason. He speaks to the frustration and anger that many people feel. People who may have good reason to fear, resent and rage about religion, and what religious people or institutions may have subjected them to. Such harm has come in many forms. Perhaps one of the less grievous forms, although bad enough, is pointed to by the poet Edwin Muir (1887–1959):

> See there King Calvin
> with his iron pen,
> And God three angry
> letters in a book[25]

This is, of course, a harsh reading of Calvin. John Calvin also had a beating heart, with its own reasons, known and unknown to himself. And, of course, to some others, Calvin has offered balm, comfort and hope. I don't discuss Calvin in this book, but if others want to tell me, in gentler tones than Edwin Muir employs, about the solace they find from Calvinism, or, for that matter, from Dawkinism, I will want to listen.

As I wrote in the opening chapter, the point is not to try to get to know more about God, or about whether or not God exists. It is, as I've already emphasised, to understand ourselves and each other better, and to learn about the different ways we get through, and get by: the different ways in which we stop ourselves walking into the sea, or, in sunnier seasons, relish the joy of swimming.

When Tony mocks Kath's belief in God, he was being an arsehole. This is not a criticism of this glorious series. Tony is supposed to be, at this point, an arsehole. This is his superpower.

Tony is an arsehole and an atheist: being this sort of arsehole is a problem, the episode affirmed, less so being an atheist.

I agree with this. I would always prefer an atheist to an arsehole.

None of my friends are arseholes. Plenty of them are atheists.

That said, I detected an off-screen seriousness at this point in the episode. It felt as if the scriptwriter (Gervais himself) was rather proud of the 'too many gods' put-down, as a piece of philosophy. Indeed, in his own writing about why he is an atheist, Gervais endorses precisely the argument deployed by Tony.[26]

I enjoyed this line of attack in *After Life* as a piece of comedy, less so as philosophy.

If it were real life, Tony should have been kinder to Kath. He should have been more curious, less dogmatic. He might have learned something he didn't already know, which, after all, is the point of conversation.

Drawing on Einstein, and on my own experience, and from empirical studies, I *know* that belief in God frequently does not involve looking for explanations, or for theories that rival science.

So, what might believing in God – in different gods (taking in the arsehole perspective here) – do for people?

Let's find out.

Talking Again

The importance of forgetting everything you thought you knew about God.

There is a story about the Indian philosopher Gandhi being asked by a journalist:

What do you think about Western civilisation?

Gandhi's reported response was:

I think it would be a good idea.[1]

The contemporary Indian philosopher Akeel Bilgrami, a professor at Columbia University, has set out the main lines of what Gandhi might have meant by this. He has in his sights the way in which a dominant strand of Western philosophy operated around certain hierarchies and binaries: male and female, property owner and slave, science and faith, knowledge and belief, nature and culture, human and non-human. The natural world – animals, rivers, glaciers, trees – came to be understood as a sheer resource, without value in itself but there to be plundered, owned and exploited. This worldview served as a justification for the exploitation of the natural world, and for colonialism.

Bilgrami expresses regret that we did not have a 'better Enlightenment': one which could have supported the growth of knowledge, science and ethics, but without stripping the world of value and enchantment.[2]

Although Bilgrami himself identifies as an atheist, he nonetheless finds that part of what happened in Western philosophy was a stripping away of a rich variety of ways – pagan, pantheist and Platonist – of talking about the divine and the world.

Bilgrami finds that from around the eighteenth century, a certain sort of overly anthropomorphic Christianity became dominant. God was conceived of as like a very powerful human being, with the living natural world having no intrinsic value, apart from what God, and other beings like God (us), might project upon it. As this type of distorted Christian perspective became more dominant, within the tradition known as Western philosophy, nothing else much was able to flourish on the forest floor. As happens in forest ecologies, in the end, this also starves the overpowering trees of the nutrients they need, until the whole ecosystem is in crisis.

In the following three chapters, I want to bring to light some philosophical ways of believing in God which have nothing much to do with Christianity, or with any traditional religion. They represent ways of believing in God, typically, which make no recourse to revelation, authority or tradition.

My way in will be through the notion of 'yearning' that I introduced in chapter 2. I outlined four types of yearning, facets of wanting to be at home in the world, that can motivate belief in God:

A yearning to address the problem of evil and suffering.

A yearning for significance, given the problem of the vastness of the universe.

A yearning for freedom, given the way in which we may feel determined by our genetics, or by vast historical and political forces.

A yearning for a type of harmony and unity in our relationships with human beings and with non-human nature, given all the clashes and fractures in perspective that we encounter.

There are plenty of excellent books, and some lousy ones, on the concept of God within the major traditional religions. There is very little said about a stream of philosophy that believes in God, without recourse to revelation, authority or tradition. When something is obscured and in the shadows, it may be a good idea to bring it into the light a little, at least to see what we think of it.

By uncovering some of the latent possibilities, some recently resurfacing, others still mostly invisible, we may take some small steps on the better road not travelled: the Enlightenment that did not evacuate the world of value and enchantment.

I look for ways of talking about God which still have *some sort* of purchase, or resonance, in the wider culture. This might be an explicit resurgence of interest in the philosophical position, with popular books and influential authors. Or, it might just be at the level of some common phrases, pieces of wisdom, or hopeful aspirations that still do work for some people. Frequently, the relationship of the idea of God to these phrases has been lost. Sketching back in the lines, linking the phrase to the idea of God, may be illuminating.

It is not the case that our only options are sheer and total atheism, or a completely committed involvement in a traditional faith, such as Christianity, Islam, Hinduism, Buddhism or Judaism.

People are funny, and there are all sorts of interesting fragments about, with deep resonances and undercurrents.

*

These positions I've chosen aren't intended to represent the full range of thought about God. Rather, they are chosen strategically to give life and movement to different fundamental options for belief in God.

One option, representing Einstein's belief in God, is where God is not something beyond or behind nature; instead God is the concept used to point to the beauty and order of the natural world. I discuss in turn Stoicism, in chapter 5 ('Being Philosophical'), and Spinozism, in chapter 6 ('Missing Out').

There are also philosophical varieties of belief in God which are not Christian, but do speak of God as a reality beyond and behind the created world. As my witness here, I discuss, in chapter 7 ('More Than This') the thought of the eighteenth-century philosopher Immanuel Kant.

Perhaps you might think that I was rather uncharitable about atheism in the previous chapter.

I don't think this is quite fair. I was hard on some atheists, with respect to the quality of their atheism, but not in terms of their undoubted ability as comedians, or popularisers of science. But atheism, like religion, is not a single category, and there are some compelling and attractive versions of it.

Just as some atheists have an impoverished understanding of religious belief, I also think that some theologians work with a truncated appreciation of how profound some types of atheism can be. Atheists are capable of much more than Richard Dawkins. To access this higher grade of atheism, I turn in chapter 8 ('Enchanting') to another facet of Akeel Bilgrami's thinking. Bilgrami reaches for an enchanted conception of nature which does not bring in the notion of the divine. The whole ecosystem here is enriched, I suggest, by bringing into the light more nuanced and capacious atheist insights. Bilgrami is an atheist who is positive about religion. I'm religious, and am positive about Bilgrami's atheism.

In my forest metaphor, I suggested that even the dominant trees suffer when the entire ecosystem is depleted, even if they are largely responsible for the depletion. The relevance for Christianity might be this: when we lose a curiosity about the types of yearning that can be at work in a variety of ways of believing in God, we also lose sight of the more profound strands in some Christian traditions. In chapter 9 ('No Greater Than'), I turn my attention to a yearning-oriented approach to a classical thinker in the Christian tradition, Anselm of Canterbury. My hope is that by coming to approach Christianity from this perspective, we might see something that couldn't be easily demolished by an advert on the side of a bus.

The final chapters of the book (10–13) consider what we do next, if, indeed, a certain type of rational argument about the existence and nature of God, or of God's non-existence, only gets us so far. I make the case, in chapter 10, for opening up about personal experiences, and unconscious and emotional forces, which can underlie our fundamental commitments. I also tackle more directly the 'variety = bollocks' theory.

If I came out religious, I was then formed and fed by Christianity, and became, and am, a Christian. In the final three chapters of the book I lean into this Christian formation. Even when operating within a single tradition, there is, of course, a great diversity of viewpoints, with passion and argument complexly intertwined.

I explore patterns of emotion-laden reasoning in relation to the question of whether we might think of God as inside (chapter 11) or outside (chapter 12) of time, or whether we find God simply absent altogether (chapter 13). All these options, shaped by freedom and desire, are aspects of the living Christian tradition.

*

The twentieth-century Christian theologian Paul Tillich writes about the 'depth and ground of all being'. Without much distortion, this maps on to my reflections about yearning, where the yearning comes from these depths. Tillich writes:

> The name of this infinite and inexhaustible depth and ground of all being is *God*. That depth is what the word *God* means. And if that word has not much meaning for you, translate it, and speak of the depths of your life, of the source of your being, of your ultimate concern, of what you take seriously

without any reservation. Perhaps, in order to do so,
you must forget everything traditional that you have
learned about God, perhaps even that word itself.[3]

This might not be bad advice.

*

A final thought: as you read some of the following chapters,
it may occur to you that in the presentation of the different
perspectives – Stoic, Spinozist, Kantian, Bilgrami's atheism,
Anselmian – *arguments* are used.

But, I thought you said arguments didn't work,
and we should go beyond them?

No, what I precisely said was that a specific type of argument – rational, abstract, atomised – did not often have the
causal effect of persuading someone to change their firmly
held conviction on the question of God.

That doesn't mean that arguments don't do anything.

They may still play a vital role. They manifest commitment, they exemplify devotion; in fact, they express desire.
Also, they put a picture, a worldview, in motion, showing
you how it moves and works. They allow you to discern
whether you find the moving picture alluring or repulsive,
or whether you find yourself rather indifferent.

It's just that arguments about God don't change minds, or prove things, in the way that a geometrical proof does. The philosophical arguments are not coercive, and they leave you with an irreducible freedom. Whether you are drawn into the argument, or repelled by it, will be down to desires and hopes that are not to be found on the face of the argument itself.

5

Being Philosophical

How believing in God makes you brave (Stoic-style).

Be philosophical about it.

This colloquial instruction – perhaps used more commonly once than it is now – is curious. It means, broadly speaking:

> Don't worry about it.
> Don't think about it.
> Don't give it another thought.
> Just get on with it.
> Don't let it bother you.
> Accept it.
> Be brave.

In this vein, I recall a doctoral student in philosophy telling me a joke, when I was planning to begin my own doctoral studies:

> Studying philosophy doesn't make you rich, but it will make you philosophical about having no money.

On first blush, this might seem a rather odd way to talk about philosophy.

After all, *thinking* and worrying about things that nobody else worries about ('could I really be dreaming?', 'how do I know the world is real?') seems to be the only thing that philosophy does do.

In fact, though, the phrase is on to something. It draws on a strand that has its roots in ancient Stoicism. Stoicism encourages us to live resignedly, and with dignity, with the warp and weft of the universe as you find it, not as you would wish it to be.

The concept of God is central for the Stoics, when they try to do this.

Furthermore, Stoicism does not posit anything that exists beyond or behind nature. God is not the explanation for nature, and God is not a supernatural entity or being.

Stoicism is making a comeback these days, with many self-help books advising readers to take it up as a way of life. Here are just a few titles you can easily find in bookshops:

The Little Book of Stoicism: Timeless Wisdom to Gain Resilience, Confidence, and Calmness

The Daily Stoic: 366 Meditations on Wisdom, Perseverance, and the Art of Living
Stoicism for Beginners

Stoicism is powerful. As these books all correctly insist, Stoicism is not about repressing emotions, but about reflecting on our feelings and gaining self-knowledge. The goal is to avoid being overwhelmed by negative emotions that do not help us to flourish, such as fear, anger and resentment.

For the most part, these books do not mention, or give much space to, the Stoic idea of God or the divine. It would probably be an embarrassment and a hindrance. It might get in the way of the urbane promises of self-improvement.

Amongst other claims in blurbs and advertising, we find the following:

Where can you find joy? Gain strength? How should we face our fears? And what about those recurring depressing thoughts?
A page-a-day guide to living a good life.
Tools and guidance to transform your life.
Discover the Way to Transform Your Life for the Better and the Path of Life-Long Success and Happiness – the Path of Stoicism!

Did you know that Stoicism is the trait of all history's successful persons and leaders?

Since 2012, there has been a global online experiment:

Live like a Stoic for a week.

The contemporary Stoic philosopher John Sellars writes that those who followed the project for a week experienced an improvement in 'their sense of wellbeing', and that those who 'followed a month-long experiment saw even greater benefits'.[1]

Let's see where, or how, the concept of God might fit into the Stoic project.

*

Take the following position:

> Nature is ordered and structured by laws. Everything in nature is ordered by these laws, and everything is complexly connected with everything else, forming a whole, which is reality. Our task, as best we can, is to study and understand these laws, and the intelligibility underlying them, and to reconcile ourselves with this reality,

> selflessly and ethically, without false consolation
> or fantasy.

I submit that this is a reasonable summary of two positions: Richard Dawkins when talking about 'the magic of reality', and Stoicism, when talking about the universe.

Consider these passages from Richard Dawkins.

> I want to show you that the real world, as under-
> stood scientifically, has magic of its own – the kind
> I call poetic magic: an inspiring beauty which is all
> the more magical because it is real and because we
> can understand how it works. Next to the true beau-
> ty and magic of the real world, supernatural spells
> and stage tricks seem cheap and tawdry by compari-
> son. The magic of reality is neither supernatural nor
> a trick, but – quite simply – wonderful. Wonderful,
> and real. Wonderful *because* real.[2]

> Rainbows are not just beautiful to look at. In a way,
> they tell us when everything began, including space
> and time. I think that makes the rainbow even more
> beautiful.[3]

In Stoic writing, there are constant invocations to attend to the 'systematic, organized unity' which makes up the world, where 'everything' is related 'to everything else'. But the unity that we find does not offer much in the way of personal comfort:

> Consider any existing object and reflect that it is
> even now in the process of dissolution and change,
> in a sense regenerating through decay or dispersal:
> in other words, to what sort of 'death' each thing is
> born.[4]

This passage comes from the *Meditations* (AD 161–80) of Marcus Aurelius, the Stoic philosopher and emperor of Rome. Marcus Aurelius loses eight children in his lifetime, five sons and three daughters. Reading his *Meditations*, it is clear that he feels such losses deeply. Stoicism, for him, is not about eliminating deep feeling, but about not being crushed, not being weighed down by resentment and bitterness. He instructs himself to avoid the prayer: 'How can I save my little child?'

Rather, he tells himself, the prayer should be:

> How can I learn not to fear his loss?[5]

The answer is not: by not loving the child.

It is through a deep and ardent acceptance, even in the most extreme circumstances.

*

Stoicism embraces the philosophical position known as the Eternal Return of the Same. This is the idea that everything that happens in the world will happen again and again, infinitely many times. The Stoic instruction here is to embrace this thought, as we live each moment, even the tedious and painful ones.

This is still a 'naturalistic' thought: there is no appeal to anything 'beyond' nature, and what structures it. Dawkins should be able to accept the Eternal Return of the Same as a possible hypothesis about reality, which does not make recourse to any supernatural beings. I accept that he would be unlikely to accept the hypothesis, unless he felt it had advantages in, say, building theories about the origins and structure of the universe. The point is, though, that it is not in itself a 'religious belief'. It is a cosmology, with ethical guidance about how to orient oneself to this cosmos. This is, in fact, a bit like Dawkins: a cosmology (Big Bang and evolution), with further ethical guidance from Dawkins about how to orient oneself to this cosmos.

The twentieth-century philosopher Pierre Hadot explains the Stoic belief in the Eternal Return of the Same:

> Universal Reason wishes this world to be as it is: that is to say, arising from the universal fire, and returning to this original fire, and therefore having a beginning and an end. Nature's will, however, is

always the same; and the only thing its continuous action can accomplish is the repetition of this world, with precisely this beginning, precisely this end, and the entire course of events situated between these two moments. Thus, this world returns equally: 'There will be another Socrates, a Plato, and every man with the same friends and the same fellow-citizens…and this renewal will not happen once, but several times; rather, all things will be repeated eternally'. This is why the sage, like universal Reason, must intensely wish for each instant: he must wish intensely for things to happen eternally exactly as they do happen.[6]

We might think about what it would mean to regard this universe, with this eternal recurrence, as divine.

*

When Stoic writers talk about the order and wholeness of this constantly changing universe, they use several terms:

Reason
Logos
The original fire
God

As we saw in chapter 3, when Einstein talks about God, he is not speaking about something beyond and behind the laws of nature. Rather, he uses the word 'God' to describe the wondrous laws of nature themselves. Stoicism is similar. Reason, Logos, the original fire, God, are all terms for the order and structure of the whole which is the universe.

Consider the ways in which Stoicism talks about God, the divine and divinity. Here is the Stoic philosopher Epictetus:

> God has made everything that is in the universe and the universe in its entirety, free of constraint and independent; but he made the parts of the Whole for the sake of the Whole. Other beings lack the capability of understanding the divine administration; but rational beings possess the inner resources which allow them to reflect upon this universe. They can reflect that they are a part of it, and on what kind of a part they are; and that it is good for the parts to yield to the Whole.[7]

When we read 'God has made everything', we may envisage a sort of designer God, creating the universe. But this wouldn't be correct. The phrase 'God has made', is a little like 'reason has determined', or 'the laws of mathematics have regulated': there is no personal, willing and loving deity.

Again, the philosopher Pierre Hadot helps illuminate the way Stoicism talks about God. Hadot writes that 'at the end of one of the periodic cycles of the Universe', God 'remains alone' because 'all things have been reabsorbed into him – that is to say, into the original fire which is at the same time the *logos* which produces the world'.[8] The concept of God, in Stoicism, seems to be a way of picking out and talking about 'at the same time', 'the original fire', 'Reason', 'Nature', the '*logos* which produces the world'.[9] Pierre Hadot, for example, talks of 'God' who is 'identical with Reason and Nature', who 'contains within himself all other seminal reasons',[10] where 'seminal reasons' generate and structure everything that is.

*

So, what is the difference that is made here, by using the concept of God?

Well, in each case, we need to be independently curious, and not assume that we know the answer before we have looked carefully.

I've suggested that when the concept of God is employed, there is often an element of yearning.

One of the types of yearning, I suggested, was in relation to evil and suffering: a desire to overcome suffering, or not be overwhelmed by it.

This seems to fit Stoicism rather well. Having 'transcended ourselves', by our ability to reflect self-consciously upon ourselves in relation to the universe/Reason/Nature/logos/ the original fire, we open ourselves up to the possibility of a sense of alienation, despair or absurdity.

But by using the concept of God to describe the universe/ Reason/Nature/logos/the original fire, we invoke in ourselves, recommend and commit ourselves to a perspective where we seek to 'cohere' with nature.

This seems to be the repeated function of the concept of the divine in Stoic writings. Saying 'God is Nature or Reason' involves a commitment to acceptance, coherence and the possibility of the elimination of the sweaty internal perspective upon ourselves – *my* projects, *my* significance, *my* concerns, *me* against the universe. Instead, we embrace a sort of external perspective upon ourselves, seeing ourselves as part of the great pattern of the universe, one with it, not separate.

In its own bracing way, Stoicism also engages with another type of yearning:

> A yearning for significance, given the problem of
> the vastness of the universe.

Reduce your desire for personal significance by lowering the temperature. Help yourself to burst out less painfully from the smallness that you are. Regard yourself simply as a moving part of the vastness.

The Stoic constantly strives to live 'coherently', with the universe and within himself:

> To live coherently – that is, according to a rule of
> life which is unique and harmonious. For those who
> live in incoherence are unhappy.[11]

Such coherence comes by attending to reality, and accepting our place within it:

> Attentive people live in the constant presence of the
> universal Reason which is immanent within the cos-
> mos. They see all things from the perspective of this
> Reason, and consent joyfully to its will.[12]

The integration is achieved without finding meaning in a 'transcendent' God or divine mind, with some sort of better, and hidden, plan for us. The concept of God picks out entirely naturalistic facts, but calling these facts God makes a difference that matters nonetheless.

As Epictetus puts it:

> This body made of mud: how could God have creat-
> ed it free of impediments? He therefore submitted it
> to the revolution of the Universe, as he did with my

> possessions, my furniture, my house, my children,
> and my wife. Why, then, should I fight against God?
> Why should I wish for things that ought not to be
> wished for?[13]

The function of 'God' here is not as an explanatory hypothesis, a theory of origins.

'God' is the entire framework within which everything that can be explained is being seen. God does not offer a consoling future for us, by which the pain of the present is justified. 'God' is a way of regarding the whole network of naturalistic facts, and my place in them.

*

The most common atheist swipe at religion is that belief in God arises from a fear of death, and a desire to have some sort of immortality.

No doubt, such fear of death is sometimes at work. But it cannot be said, here, in relation to the way in which Stoics talk about God.

Marcus Aurelius is clear about our mortality:

> In man's life his time is a mere instant, his existence
> a flux, his perception fogged, his whole bodily com-
> position rotting, his mind a whirligig, his fortune
> unpredictable, his fame unclear. To put it shortly: all

> things of the body stream away like a river, all things of the mind are dreams and delusion; life is warfare, and a visit in a strange land; the only lasting fame is oblivion.[14]

Marcus Aurelius asks:

> What then can escort us on our way? One thing, and one thing only: philosophy.

And what does philosophy consist in?

> This consists in keeping the divinity within us inviolate and free from harm, master of pleasure and pain, doing nothing without aim, truth, or integrity, and independent of others' actions or failure to act. Further, accepting all that happens and is allotted to it as coming from that other source which is its own origin: and at all times awaiting death with the glad confidence that it is nothing more than the dissolution of the elements of which every living creature is composed. Now if there is nothing fearful for the elements themselves in their constant changing of each into another, why should I only look anxiously in prospect at the change and dissolution of them all? This is in accordance with nature: and nothing harmful is in accordance with nature.[15]

God, in this scheme, is not something that will rescue us from our death. God is the gathering concept we go to, when exhorting ourselves to face our death. If you keep the 'divinity' within you 'inviolate':

> You strip away many unnecessary troubles which lie wholly in your own judgement. And you will immediately make large and wide room for yourself by grasping the whole universe in your thought, contemplating the eternity of time, and reflecting on the rapid change of each thing in every part – how brief the gap from birth to dissolution, how vast the gulf of time before your birth, and an equal infinity after your dissolution.[16]

*

Most of the recent self-help books on Stoicism don't have anything to do with the concept of God or the divine. It is cut out of the texts.

Censored.

And, yet, it was central for the Stoics themselves.

Why has God been removed from the picture?

Again, there has been a reduction in the breadth and depth of our appreciation for all that can be contained by the concept of God.

We are offered a thin gruel, dominated, often, in the public understanding by superstition, fundamentalism, and sentimentality. There is dogmatism on all sides, theist and atheist.

Whatever we think of this, it is not what vast swathes of many philosophical or theological traditions have meant when talking about God. There is a huge sloughing off of cultural memory and self-consciousness.

Are we happy with this forgetting and/or censoring?

Does it help us?

Someone might put the question back to me.

Well, why not?

What harm does it do?

*

One type of harm might arise from a type of avoidable ignorance: that when someone projects an anthropomorphic God concept onto all historical uses of the term God, this blinds us to the depth and possibilities of those uses.

This creates a self-satisfied arrogance about the past, and all the people in the past, who have believed in God. If we think we know what they meant by 'God', and we wrongly assume that they meant something stupid and intolerant, it is we who have become stupid and intolerant.

Furthermore, it creates a self-satisfied arrogance about other people in the present, who might believe in God, or talk about God. Stoicism, for example, is a huge presence in Christian belief and philosophy, not only in the scholarly tradition, but also at a mainstream cultural level. Take the beginning of John's Gospel:

> In the beginning was the Word, and the Word was with God. (Jn. 1:1)

'Word' is the translation for the Stoic term *Logos:* evoking reason, the original fire, God.

To announce a new resurgence of Stoicism, as if it had simply disappeared until now, is to say something a little ignorant about what Christianity is, in its past and present.

But is there more we can say here?

Is there a sense in which God is, in fact, an integral concept in Stoicism, one that it cannot easily do without? Without the God concept, would it be Stoicism? Albeit, of course, that the Stoic God concept is different to the Christian God.

Why does God matter?

What difference, that matters, does God make to the world?

To help us to think about this, I'm going to employ a distinction, sometimes used by philosophers, between facts and concepts.

Different concepts can pick out the same facts: for example, 'H_2O' and 'water' are different concepts, but the statements 'there is some water' and 'there is some H_2O'

both pick out the same naturalistic state of affairs. That they are different concepts should be clear: people were speaking about the clear, colourless liquid in our seas and rivers long before we knew anything about molecular structure.

It matters, in different contexts, which concept we use. Take Philip Larkin's poem 'Water':

> If I were called in
> To construct a religion
> I should make use of water
> … I should raise in the east
> A glass of water
> Where any-angled light
> Would congregate endlessly.

Then replace 'water' with H_2O. It doesn't work.

> If I were called in
> To construct a religion
> I should make use of H_2O
> … I should raise in the east
> A glass of H_2O…

'Water' evokes the whole rhythm of life, birth and death, thirst and satiety, ritual and cleansing, swimming, childhood baths, the sea, showers, hot tubs and drowning. H_2O is for chemistry lessons.

Which concepts we choose to use, or are chosen for us, makes a difference, even when we are talking about the same set of facts.

*

John Sellars, in his introduction to Stoicism, writes about 'the Stoic's God'. For the Stoics, he writes, God is 'identified with the animating rational principle in Nature':

> Their God is not a person but rather a physical principle that accounts for the order and organization of the natural world. When Seneca refers to the 'will of God', then, he is referring to this organizing principle, which the Stoics identified with fate...Stoic fate is the fate of physics, not superstition.[17]

This is correct, of course, as far as it goes.

The facts are the facts of Stoic physics. We have a choice of which concept to employ when orienting ourselves to these facts: God or an 'animating rational principle'; water or H_2O.

What difference might be made by using the concept 'God', and what might be lost if we lose this concept?

Perhaps the concept of divinity has something to do with yearning, a desire for a proper relationship with what is called God?

Here I come back to the notion of 'yearning'. I have suggested that Stoicism might particularly address two types of yearning:

A yearning to address the problem of evil and suffering.
A yearning for significance, given the problem of the vastness of the universe.

Using the concept of God does not add another thing to the picture. Instead, it invokes and puts into motion our living relationship to the whole. When the Stoic uses the concept of God, she announces, to herself and others, that she wishes to be transformed, healed, to be made large in spirit, by embracing and accepting the smallness of our lives, and the greatness of the cosmos in which we participate.

*

At the end of his book on Stoicism, Sellars writes the following:

We can, I hope, all benefit from thinking about the issues that the Stoics addressed. But the real benefit comes, they would insist, only if we incorporate these ideas into our daily lives. This is where the really hard work begins.[18]

I might add: the difference made by using the word God, or entering the space which the word would fill, is the choice to undertake this hard work, with an element of unsentimental hope.

Without the hard work, and the crushed yearning, Stoicism may not be much more than a cheery and unrealistic fridge magnet.

Missing Out

How to cope with FOMO by believing in God (Spinoza-style).

As with varying reactions to wasp and bee stings – from itchiness to anaphylactic shock – the fear of missing out (FOMO) can be anything from a minor irritant to a life-limiting and life-threatening condition.

I know someone who will only ever order what his partner is ordering, even if it is not his preferred meal. The anticipated pleasure from having what he would prefer never outweighs his terror of food envy, the fear of missing out. Others will make themselves go to parties, holidays, meetings, whatever, not because they positively want to, but out of fear of the suffering which is FOMO, or, even worse, perhaps, its realised state, knowledge of missing out (KOMO).

Both FOMO and KOMO can also be terribly serious.

So much yearning and suffering can arise for us because of a sense of the path not taken, the 'imagined otherwise', the life not lived, the universe in which this or that loss did not occur, in which we could be with this person, or could have chosen this career, or could have said, or done, this thing, and not another.[1]

In this universe not inhabited, we may see ourselves as more whole, more entire, more alive, less injured, physically or psychically.

The thought of this other life can bring comfort and excitement, through a sort of fantasy and illusion, but it may also, in the end, or even the beginning, bring pain and suffering, and a depletion of energy and imagination to live here and now, in this life.

What if we could entirely excise both FOMO and KOMO from our lives? Would this help? And what, if anything, would this have to do with God?

When something difficult or painful happens, you can sometimes hear people say:

Everything happens for a reason.

This fragment of speech has tendrils that may take us back to the God of Spinoza.

*

In chapter 3, we came across Einstein's announcement:

I believe in Spinoza's God, who reveals himself in the orderly harmony of what exists.[2]

I promised to come back to Einstein's concept of 'Spinoza's God', and to unpack what this might mean. This is where I cash in on that promise.

Baruch Spinoza (1632–77) was born and raised in the Portuguese-Jewish community of Amsterdam. Because of his controversial ideas, he was expelled from this community at the age of twenty-three by the Jewish religious authorities. He lived an outwardly modest life, rejecting awards and prestigious teaching appointments. He worked, instead, as an optical lens grinder, dying at the age of forty-four from a lung illness, possibly caused by inhaling glass dust.

A year after his death, the Protestant states of Holland banned his entire works, on the grounds that:

> [T]hey contain very many profane, blasphemous and atheistic propositions.

In an ecumenical gesture, the Catholic Church added Spinoza's works to the Index of Forbidden Books a year later, in 1679.

One of Spinoza's most famous lines is where he talks about the whole of everything that exists, and calls it 'God or Nature'.[3]

I have been asking, in this book, what might really be going on when two people regard the same set of 'facts', and one of them reaches for the concept of God, and the other for the concept of nature (with no God).

God or Nature.

I will explore one interpretation of the set of facts that Spinoza thinks he is dealing with, and then consider what it might mean to invoke or to reject the concept of God, in relation to this set of facts.

The brief sketch of his life, and immediate afterlife – being banned by a synagogue and a number of churches – is a clear indication that Spinoza did not believe in the God of Judaism or Christianity. Spinoza's God is not a personal and providential God, to whom you can pray, or whom you should ask for personal help and guidance.

If not a 'who', *what* then is Spinoza's God?

*

I am going to draw on an interpretation offered by Rebecca Newberger Goldstein, not because I think it is the correct account of Spinoza – on this, I offer no view – but because it serves a distinct purpose for my argument. Spinoza can be read as an atheist, or as a pantheist, where God is nature, or as something approaching a more traditional monotheist, with God as somehow separate from the world.[4]

Goldstein reads Spinoza as a pantheist, with a focus on Spinoza's bracing determinism and fatalism.

The most striking thing about the Spinozistic attitude to facts is not so much which facts obtain, but the aspiration that surrounds facts. As Goldstein puts it, the 'fundamental intuition' is:

> [T]he demand that all facts come with an account-
> ing so complete as to rule out the very possibility
> that they might not have been facts.[5]

This needs the sort of 'accounting that we get in mathe-matics, all corners squarely tucked into deduction'.[6] She explains that 'existence comes in only two flavours: neces-sary or impossible':

> We are denizens of the only possible world. An al-
> ternative to it cannot be and cannot be conceived.[7]

Let us tackle the two terms: 'necessary' and 'impossible'.

'Impossible' is easier to grasp, so we will begin there. If you hear a philosopher talking about something being im-possible – and if they are saying this qua being a philosopher, and not just when complaining at a meeting, you need to ask what they mean.

Some philosophers will reserve the term 'impossible' for what is called the logically impossible. Something is logi-cally impossible only if it involves a straight contradiction, of the form '*a* and *not a*'. A favourite example in the philo-sophical literature is the married bachelor. Where 'bachelor' means 'unmarried man', we can see that it is an impossible self-contradiction.

Philosophers who have this sort of account of impossibility don't just mean that it is extremely unlikely, or vanishingly improbable. Consider all the following scenarios. All of them, in a philosophical sense, would usually be regarded as 'possible', even if highly unlikely:

You will marry into the royal family (if you are a royal reader, this example won't work for you).
You will win the lottery jackpot four times.
You will travel to Mars one day.
A free human being will never do anything that is wrong or unkind.

They are *possible*, just because there does not seem to be any actual contradiction of the form '*a* and *not a*' involved in affirming them.

But we might wonder if there are other types of absolute impossibility – not just 'extreme unlikelihood' – operating, which go beyond logical impossibility, which are impossible because they generate other types of difficulty. Are there deep structures and limitations on what is really possible, even if we cannot catch them by sniffing out contradictions?

Spinoza thinks that the whole universe is deeply patterned and structured with such limitations on what is really possible, from top to bottom, and at every level, in ways that go far beyond mere logical impossibility. It is difficult to give examples here, precisely because we are only equipped to grasp logical impossibilities.

We might explore the final example in the list I set out above:

> A free human being will never do anything that is
> wrong or unkind.

This proposition has got some philosophers of religion excited.

As I say, it is only one possible example. Spinoza would think that the laws about deep impossibilities are at work everywhere: in the structure of atoms and amoebas, and in the flow of traffic in a city centre. Let's work, though, with this one.

The possibility that a free human being might never do anything wrong or unkind is an interesting one, with wide ramifications for some debates around the 'problem of evil'.

Perhaps it is actually impossible for there to be a free finite human being, who enjoys such freedom, but who never does anything wrong or unkind. There is no 'a and not-a' type of contradiction here, but just something deep about the interaction of being human (and therefore finite), and being free. Being finite, with limited resources for altruism and fairness, and being free – and therefore capable of choosing one thing over another – sometimes you will have to squash, or overlook, something, or someone, at least for a bit.

Sure, you're only human.

We sometimes say something along these lines, and we all sort of understand.

Consider a standard presentation of the 'problem of evil':

1. God is all-powerful.
2. God is perfectly good.
3. If God were all-powerful and perfectly good, God would have the ability and desire not to permit the existence of evil and suffering.
4. There is evil and suffering.
5. Therefore, God either does not exist, or is not all-powerful, or not perfectly good.

But, if it is *really impossible* – as impossible as a square circle or a married bachelor – for God to create free finite beings who never do wrong, or act unkindly, then we might be able to attack the third move here, where it is affirmed that 'God would have the ability and desire not to permit the existence of evil and suffering'. Perhaps, not even God would have the ability to create free finite beings who never do wrong, just as God could not create a square circle, not because of a lack of power or goodness, but because such a thing just isn't a thing that can be done.

The only question, then, is whether it would be better never to have created finite beings with freedom at all. Maybe the creation of anything finite will involve some sort of pain. So, then, the debate becomes: would it have been better if there had been nothing finite at all?

We could argue about this, but it is a different question.

If we argue that it would be better if there had been nothing at all, are we turkeys voting for Christmas? Not quite.

We are more like turkeys fearing Christmas so much that they vote to wind up the whole of creation, all of space and time. I think for some people, some of the time, this is an understandable reaction to what they are given, but it will be great suffering and personal experience, one suspects, that will deliver this vote, and not a philosophical argument.

*

So much for impossibility; what about necessity?

A state of affairs is impossible if there is no possible world, no possible universe, where that state of affairs could exist. A state of affairs, or a truth, is necessary if it has to pertain, or to be true, in every and any possible world.

If we know that some states of affairs are impossible, we already know that some things are necessary.

This is an easier thought than might initially appear.

If it is impossible to have a square circle, or a married bachelor, we know the following:

Necessarily, there are no square circles.
Necessarily, there are no married bachelors.

More controversially, depending on what we said about the example of freedom, finitude and evil, we may also say:

Necessarily, there are no free human beings who never do anything that is wrong or unkind.

What are we saying with this assertion?
We are saying:

Whenever there is a world with finite and self-conscious beings in it, those finite and self-conscious beings will always, somehow, at some time, act in ways that are wrong or unkind.

What if, though, as with laws about impossibility, the web of necessary truths was woven throughout the entire universe, explaining the structure and characteristics of *everything*, from all sorts of life forms to the behaviour of stars and planetary systems?

We might not ever be able to fathom, or work out, what these necessary truths are, but we could come to be convinced, perhaps by philosophy, that these necessary truths exist, and that they structure, shape and explain everything.

At the most maximal end of things, we might even think that it is necessary that this universe exists: it had to exist, as certainly as the truth that if there is a triangle, its internal angles add up to 180 degrees.

We are now approaching Spinoza's worldview, as explained by Goldstein:

> Existence comes in only two flavours: necessary or impossible.

We are denizens of the only possible world. An alternative to it cannot be and cannot be conceived.[8]

This is a claim of staggering proportions. Try to imagine yourself believing it, and feel what happens to your perspective on things. (Maybe you do believe it, in which case, you don't need to imagine.)

> It therefore follows that, if a given number of individual things exist in nature, there must be some cause for the existence of exactly that number, neither more nor less. For example, if twenty men exist in the universe (for simplicity's sake, I will suppose them existing simultaneously, and to have had no predecessors), and we want to account for the

existence of these twenty men, it will not be enough
to show the cause of human existence in general; we
must also show why there are exactly twenty men,
neither more nor less; for a cause must be assigned
for the existence of each individual.[9]

This should be extended to 'everything whatsoever' for
which 'a cause or reason must be assigned, either for its existence, or for its non-existence'. As Spinoza puts the point
in *Ethics*:

[I]f a triangle exists, a reason or cause must be granted for its existence; if, on the contrary, it does not
exist, a cause must also be granted, which prevents it
from existing, or annuls its existence...But the reason for the existence of a triangle or a circle does not
follow from the nature of those figures, but from
the order of universal nature in extension. From the
latter it must follow, either that a triangle necessarily
exists, or that it is impossible that it should exist.
So much is self-evident. It follows therefrom that
a thing necessarily exists, if no cause or reason be
granted which prevents its existence.[10]

We have here a radical extension of what Gottfried Wilhelm
Leibniz called the 'Principle of Sufficient Reason'. This principle insists:

> [N]o fact could ever be true or existent, no state-
> ment correct, unless there were a sufficient reason
> why it was thus and not otherwise – even though
> those reasons will usually not be knowable by us.[11]

Spinoza goes beyond Leibniz in claiming:

> [T]he world itself offers up its own complete ex-
> planation, crowding out the very possibility of a
> transcendent God, a God whose choices offer expla-
> nations for the world from *outside* the world.[12]

Why do you live at number 18 on your street, and not number 25? This is as necessary as the properties of a geometric
shape. Why were you born?

> It was necessary, and anything else was
> impossible.

Why did this or that wonderful or terrible event befall you?

> It was necessary, and anything else was
> impossible.

Why did I waste so many years of my life on this career/
addiction/partner?

It was necessary, and anything else was impossible.

Why didn't I choose the butternut risotto with toasted porcini shavings?

It was necessary, and anything else was impossible.

This isn't my worldview, but when I imaginatively occupy it, I do find that it has both a bracing and liberating affect.

It is radically non-judgemental. It encourages a lack of resentment. It deflates lament. It also removes hope. Hope, of course, can be a source of tremendous pain and suffering. At its peak, this worldview breathes a deep 'Yes' to everything that is, and has been, in an extraordinary acceptance and affirmation that, in spite of it all, this is what had to happen.

If there being something, and not nothing, is good, then everything and anything, in some sense, is good.

Quite a big 'if', perhaps, for some.

*

Where does God come into all of this?

First of all, we should consider the types of 'facts' we have, and then what might be at stake in calling this whole set of facts

'God', or 'nature', or, as Spinoza does, 'God or Nature', apparently embracing a type of conceptual pluralism or ambivalence.

As Goldstein describes it, the facts in front of us are:

> [A] whole infinite set of…explanations *in toto* [as a whole], bound all together by the internal necessity connecting causes and effects by way of laws which are themselves ultimately explicable, [and] necessary.[13]

If we call all this 'the world', we can ask, in turn, what *accounts* for the world in its entirety.

Goldstein suggests that three types of candidate present themselves:[14]

1. Something, traditionally known as *God*, that exists outside the world.
2. Something that exists within the world.
3. The world itself.

The first two candidates will not satisfy Spinoza.

Take the first candidate: a God existing outside the world. For Spinoza, what it is to be part of the world just is to be part of the nexus of things that can be fully explained. If something is outside of the world, it is outside of the network of full explanations, and it is inexplicable, incoherent and, therefore, non-existent.

The second type of candidate – 'something that exists within the world' – is even less promising: nothing within reality could explain the 'whole infinite totality', precisely because any single part of reality is only what it is by 'dragging in a massive tangle of entailments', reaching out again into the whole world.[15]

The only possible candidate is option three, 'the world itself':

> This gives us an exquisite solution, with a mathematical elegance devoutly to be desired. The thing which accounts for the world itself is the world itself. It is the world, understood as the infinite implicate order containing all explanations.[16]

Goldstein reflects that this is not 'an argument which runs on definitions', but rather on the 'fundamental intuition' that 'all facts come with an accounting'.[17]

What Spinoza envisages is 'an implicate order of a complexity so vast, involving abstractions so subtle, that it is, in its absolute being, hidden to our incurably finite and concrete minds':

> What we know of it is that it is so compelling as to bring about its own existence. This compellingness is what constitutes its essence [that it exists and how

it exists], a coiled necessity that explodes in an infinity of consequences.[18]

What is promised is a Final Theory of Everything:[19]

> Spinoza is asserting that there is a Final Theory of Everything, which, accounting, as it promises, for *everything*, will also account for why it itself is the Final Theory of Everything. It provides the explanation for itself. It is, in Spinoza's language, the *causa sui* [cause of itself]…arbitrariness is ultimately to be expelled from the universe.[20]

*

Goldstein explicitly turns to the choice of whether or not to use the word 'God' here.

> What kind of name is that for a Final Theory of Everything? Why start using that term to refer to the implicate order?[21]

Goldstein's answer is brisk, exciting and a little alarming, or so I find. 'Well', she writes, 'why not' use the word of God?

> [J]ust so long as one carefully guards against illegitimately smuggling in any …characteristics

associated with more conventional notions of God.[22]

She goes on to reflect:

> The notion of the whole vast sweep of existence, itself necessarily existing and providing in itself the complete explanation for everything, is sufficiently impressive to be appropriately called God, if you're hankering to call something or other God.[23]

So far, then, we have mainly weak psychological permission: why not call it God, Goldstein asks, if you have a 'hankering' to do so?

The word 'hankering' troubles me: doesn't it imply something slightly neurotic and clingy?

I'd prefer to say 'yearn'.

When I say that Goldstein's suggestion is alarming and exciting, I have in mind her relative insouciance, her urbane indifference to the question.

Goldstein is happy enough with the use of the God concept, but also relatively unfazed by it, almost unbothered. The word 'God', Goldstein comments, 'doesn't add anything substantive' to Spinoza's universe, 'nothing over and above what is already implied by' the 'fundamental intuition' that everything has an entire necessary explanation, where any other universe is ruled as impossible:

> [A]ll facts come with an accounting so complete as
> to rule out the very possibility that they might not
> have been facts.

Immediately after this, Goldstein goes on to consider a slightly more 'positive' thought:

> [P]erhaps Spinoza thought the use of the term
> 'God'…would do some good, underlining the fact
> that no *other* God – a transcendent God, with all
> sorts of inscrutable designs, making us half-mad
> with desperation to discover what his intentions for
> us are and thereby save ourselves – was possible: the
> position of God has already been filled; no others
> need apply.[24]

This 'negative' suggestion is an interesting one: that Spinoza mainly wants to blackball other more ambitious or substantial uses of the concept of God.

*

In relation to Goldstein's bracing reflections, we might circle back around to FOMO and KOMO.

First of all, we might challenge the claim that nothing much is added to a picture if we choose to use a different concept to describe the same set of facts. I've already said something about this in the previous chapter, in relation to Stoicism.

What, then, might be added by using the concept of God?

The invitation being offered in the option to call nature 'God', on Goldstein's reading of Spinoza, seems to me to be a radical overcoming of FOMO and KOMO. This is a more serious suggestion than it might sound. We've discussed how much suffering the 'imagined otherwise' can cause us. In this universe not inhabited, we see ourselves as more whole, less damaged, happier, freer.

The bracing consolation offered by Spinozism is that everything that happens is necessary, in that it is impossible that it could have been otherwise – 'a coiled necessity that explodes in an infinity of consequences'.[25]

We can forget about 'sliding doors'-type fantasies: from the film where entirely different lives unfold depending on whether or not you manage to get through the sliding doors onto the train in time. There was only ever going to be one outcome.

Does this help?

Well, maybe, for some.

It might help to the extent that our pain and disintegration is associated with a lack of explanation for sorrow and suffering, and a sense that things might have been better. Is the naming of this God compulsory? I would suggest not. But it can be powerful.

Some people are powerfully drawn to Spinoza's fatalism, such as Einstein:

> I believe in Spinoza's God, who reveals himself in
> the orderly harmony of what exists.[26]

*

I'll admit, in the spirit of revealing emotional reactions to formal arguments, as well as conscious rational objections, that Spinozism can rile me. It 'gets my goat', a little bit. Perhaps it would be more accurate to say that I can react, with negative affect, to a certain sort of superior self-satisfaction that some Spinozists exude – or that I project upon them – even though I might like these same people very much, when they are not being smug about Spinoza.

What is it that irritates?

On the one hand, I am told that I am causally determined, that all my errors, follies and virtues are fate, along with everything that befalls me: blessings, accidents, tedium, administration all included.

All fate.

I can understand this, although I'm not sure I agree.

But then there is a zeal in the presentation of the ideas, an encouragement to me, a recommendation for a way of life, sometimes almost a hectoring:

> You will become much happier and more
> consoled if you can accept this fate without re-
> sentment, with a joyful 'Yes!', a dance.

Do it.

Say 'Yes!

Try, at least.

But now, I am puzzled.

Who is the 'you' being addressed here?

It seems that as well as God being a 'what', and not a 'who', I have become a 'what' also. It is often emphasised that Spinoza's God is not 'personal', because his God does not have a will, or freedom.

But for Spinoza, people do not have a proper will, or any freedom, either. If the lack of these properties makes God impersonal, why not us, too?

If Spinoza's fatalism is correct, what have *I* got to do with whether or not I am convinced of Spinoza's fatalism, and whether or not I can embrace this fatalism without resentment?

These things are fatalistically determined: what is the point of you trying to persuade me? Somehow, I'm just not involved anymore. I'm annihilated.

But I don't want to be annihilated, and I want freedom.

I certainly don't want to be told to be happy about the annihilation and lack of freedom.

It is as if I am watching a television drama, but then, suddenly, one of the characters talks to camera, breaking the fourth wall:

Do something about the imminent murder!

The character commands me.

Don't just sit there!

I feel stirred up, hectored, but then the episode continues to unravel inevitably.

What was the point in hectoring me?

I know, by the way, that you can't help hectoring me either: you are part of the unravelling, already-made episode. It's not really your fault.

People who love and know Spinoza tell me I'm looking at things the wrong way: 'not getting it'.

I'm sure this is correct.

But, I suppose, that I don't get it is fated also. If I do come to get it, by virtue of you explaining it to me, or through the power of your emotional witness, well, this will be fated also. At a certain level, it feels to me, 'I' needn't get involved.

*

What I've presented here is not simply an argument against Spinoza. It is a confession of a limitation in my understanding, along with something of a negative emotional reaction.

What my emotional reaction reveals is how important, for me, a type of freedom is that *belongs to me*. I have to feel *in it*, somehow.

What I'd like to hear and understand next, from the Spinozist, is how things are and feel for him or her, and, perhaps what he or she fears or finds repulsive, or baffling, in my desire for freedom and involvement in my life.

I've mentioned my own reaction here, because it is relevant to the question I posed at the head of this part of the book:

What is it that arguments do?

My reaction to the argument is pretty visceral. I can get genuinely irritated: my heartbeat gets faster, I redden in the face, my breathing gets shallower, I find myself digging my fingernails into the palm of my hand. The irritation has nothing to do with a mistake in the abstract progression of the argument.

But I'm glad the argument is out there. It displays the position, and enables me to orient myself in relation to it. It is a bit like choosing, and reacting to, clothes, including choosing whether or not to care much about clothes, which is also a statement and communication.

When people put forward arguments, they are getting dressed for the day, going out in the world. We react differently to people, depending on their clothes and mannerisms. We can't help it. Different things happen, of course, when people undress. Sometimes it makes us feel more humane towards them, more compassionate and understanding of their shared vulnerability.

*

With Spinozism, we have another variety of religious belief and commitment: something so bracing that it can hardly be called hope, but where the final and necessary death of hope itself brings a type of peace, and this is called God.

Or, at least, in Goldstein's formulation:

Why not call it God?

The *casualness* of Goldstein's question haunts me a little.

There is a sort of 'sure, whatever' tone to this.

In the previous chapter, I explored the extent to which the concept of God might be of central importance to the hard work that Stoicism calls us to. With Spinozism, I'm not so confident that God is so central or irreducible. How could it be, if Goldstein can be so indifferent to the terminology?

The relative lack of urgency to the God concept would seem to be borne out in the way in which Spinozists can draw authentically on Spinoza, and be profoundly atheist, or...not:

God or Nature.

This sort of insouciance also unsettles me.

I'm unsure whether it manifests a type of indifference, or an enviable ability to hold the tension of a deep ambivalence.

In any case, and for right or wrong, I know that I need something more.

More Than This

How to believe in 'something more' without losing your reason (Kant-style).

When people describe 'Western' values, either to celebrate or to critique them, a particular cluster of words is likely to come to the fore, including, perhaps, some of the following: freedom, individualism, rights, duties, secularism and, maybe, atheism.

The philosopher most often associated with this set of aspirations is Immanuel Kant (1724–1804).

Kant's notion of freedom and of individual dignity is frequently asserted to be one of the cornerstones of Western values, undergirding UN charters and assumptions in jurisprudence and medical ethics.

In this chapter, I'm going to show you the deeply spiritual and transcendent origins, in Kant's thought, of some of these assumptions and values.

Kant is not what he seems to be, and nor is the world, for Kant, what it seems to be. It is far more than it seems to be, in a way that deeply involves God. If it were not, Kant thinks we would be in serious trouble.

*

With Stoic and Spinozistic conceptions of God it was possible to identify a type of thought, even just a fragment or a phrase, that one can hear others say, or find in one's own mind at times:

It was meant to be.
Everything happens for a reason.
Be philosophical about it.

A Kantian spark or shard might be discerned in some of the following phrases:

There has to be more to life than just this.
I believe in 'something else' – something more to life.
We don't really know what is really going on, or what fundamental reality is really like.
When listening to this piece of music, or watching the sunset over the sea, I felt a sense of deep recognition and belonging. Something myself, but beyond myself.

Something of a Kantian spiritual frisson might be activated, perhaps, when we pick up a fragment of cutting-edge physics, which tells us that our conceptions of three-dimensional space and linear time may not be true of the universe all the way down.

Strikingly, a number of scholars, such as T. R. V. Murti, have commented on the affinities between strands of Kant's philosophy and the Madhyamaka school of Buddhist thought, where fundamental reality is conceived of as being radically different from how it appears.

*

When I first came across the figure of Kant, this wasn't quite how he was presented.

In my student years (1993–2000), the figure of Immanuel Kant loomed large: a little menacing maybe, but more, perhaps, as a sort of killjoy.

Kant had created real problems for theology, and for our ability to speak at all about God. Kant had thrown down a gauntlet, by claiming that *all* talk about God is without justification, whether such talk comes from people who believe, or from atheists. For this reason, there were endless articles and essays on the 'problem of God-talk', as it was called. It's not just belief in God that is problematic, but all speech about God. A theologian who might become convinced by Kant couldn't even retrain as an atheist: 'God-talk' was out. *Verboten*.

I'm going to use the next few paragraphs to paraphrase what we might call 'the Kantian challenge':

> To have a justified belief, you need to have a combination of concepts and experience. If you just have experience, with no conceptual structures

to it, you will have a formless and unintelligible mess. If you just have concepts, with no grounding experience, you will have unjustified beliefs: fairy tales and imagination.

God, by definition, is beyond space and time. So, when it comes to God, we only have concepts and never experiences.

If you experience something, it is, by definition, in space and time. Therefore, it cannot be God.

It will never be possible to have justified belief in God, because we can never have the required experiences.

Something like the Kantian challenge – a lite version of it – can be found in humanistic and atheistic put-downs of religion, from figures such as Richard Dawkins and Ricky Gervais. At times they even cite Kant as an ally and ancestor. What these atheists tend to suppress is that the Kantian ban also extends to all varieties of God-talk, including atheism.

This sort of Kantian challenge is an indiscriminate weed-killer not only for theology (and atheism), but for many of the other ambitions of philosophy. The challenge will be a hindrance for anyone who wants to say something ambitious about reality (beyond empirical observation), or goodness, or beauty.

Another thing that is widely known about Kant is that he was keen on you doing your duty: obeying universal rules regardless of whether things go well for you, or whether this produces happiness.

The whole picture was a rather grim one, with damp and dreary demands for responsibility all around: don't do that, don't believe that, don't...

Sometimes, when thinkers were less keen on Kant, he could morph from being just a killjoy into something more menacing and dangerous. This could happen when the focus was on what was regarded as his overdemanding concept of freedom, or his unrealistic expectations about our power and rationality. This sort of worry about Kant is set out by Iris Murdoch, for example, when she compares the ideal Kantian subject with the figure of Lucifer in Milton's *Paradise Lost*:

> ...free, independent, lonely, powerful, rational, responsible, brave, the hero of so many novels and books of moral philosophy...the offspring of the age of science, confidently rational and yet increasingly aware of his alienation from the material universe which his discoveries reveal.[1]

It is all the more grimly impressive that Kant manages to cast this dark dust cloud over Europe without stepping further than twenty miles from his local Prussian city of Königsberg, now called Kaliningrad, and part of Russia. The standard anecdotes about Kant emphasise his love of unadventurous habit: the same walk at the same time of day, with citizens of Königsberg able to set their clocks by observing when he walked by, with his faithful – although sometimes intoxicated (but not on the walks) – servant Lampe walking a measured distance behind, carrying an umbrella, in case it was needed.

Kant, out of principle, apparently smoked just one pipeful of tobacco a day, in the early morning. Some friends claimed that each time he purchased a new pipe, it was larger than the last.

At a point in my life, I was so troubled by the Kantian challenge – killjoy and danger – as I understood it, that I decided to spend a lot of time researching him, and thinking about his relationship to theology, and to God-talk. I spent about fifteen years turning myself into a 'Kant scholar', and I came up with a distinctive interpretation of what I think Kant is really doing.

One of the things that I found was that the best critic of the 'Kantian challenge' was in fact *Kant himself.*

The Kantian challenge is something that Kant himself would take apart and refuse to engage with. That is to say: the 'Kantian challenge' is what has arisen in the minds of some of his readers and admirers, even though Kant is a long way from thinking in these terms at all. Kant does not think, as I will show, that justified belief in God is impossible. He thinks we ought to believe in God, and that it is irrational not to do so.

This sort of thing is more common than you might think: where the impact of a body of work is diametrically opposed to what the thinker intended. Perhaps we recognise this from ordinary life and conversation. When someone succeeds in framing an original or creative thought, their words might set hares running in the minds of others, and take them in directions that were not intended by the original speaker. And, sometimes, implausible interpretations of the same speaker's intentions can gain considerable traction and become influential. This could be because of a desire to hold aloft the admired thinker, the source of our inspiration, and, perhaps, to bask in their reflective prestige. If we hold them high enough, and make enough noise, we might not hear their protestations that this isn't what they meant or wanted at all.

*

It was around 2008 when I returned to a serious study of Kant, after quite a lot of him as a student.

It was a good time to do this.

Interpretations of Kant had moved on a bit since the 1990s. Many philosophers and intellectual historians had started to think that Kant had no interest in setting the 'Kantian challenge', or that, if he did, he constantly failed to meet it.[2] These readings of Kant found that he himself wanted to say quite ambitious things: about fundamental reality (beyond empirical observation), about goodness, and about beauty. Some commentators were even able to admit that Kant wanted to say quite a lot, perhaps, about God.

I joined this intellectual wave, of rethinking and rereading Kant, with a particular interest in what Kant had to say about God, in relation to the issue of human freedom.

My most distinctive claim, perhaps, is that although Kant believes in God and transcendence, he consciously diverges from Christianity as he would have received it. Kant avoids the categories of revelation, tradition and authority. He also rejects the traditional claim that loving and knowing God is our highest good.[3] He wants to enjoy a participation in freedom and reason that are themselves divine, rather than receiving grace or salvation from an external reality. Also, Kant does not think that the historical figure of Jesus of Nazareth was uniquely divine or revelatory.

Perhaps even more strikingly, Kant believes that our true freedom only exists beyond space and time. We, each of us, as free individuals, exist beyond and outside of space and time. In this way, we share features of the life of God.

Simply jumping to the conclusion – 'freedom occurs beyond and behind space and time' – often does not achieve much beyond a baffled stare:

> Really?
> How does that help?
> Why say *that*?

It helps, I find, to come at the issue from quite a long way off, as if doing a slow zoom on Google Earth. We need to understand

Kant's deep motivation for his position. My explanation of this deep motivation will come in two parts. First of all, I will describe Kant's problem, as he understands it. I'm going to suggest that you think of this as an 'escape room'. If you have ever done an escape room, you will know that you have a set amount of time to solve various puzzles. If you are successful, you are released. During this time, you are fed clues. Accordingly, after setting up the escape room, I will provide you with four clues, or four principles of Kant's philosophy, which, when combined in the correct way, enable Kant to be released from the trap he is in. I'll show you how he does this.

*

If you were to visit contemporary Kaliningrad, a seaport on the Russian Baltic coast, you might take in Immanuel Kant's gravestone. If you did, you would read the following words, quoted from his work:

> Two things fill the mind with ever new and increasing admiration and reverence, the more often and more steadily one reflects on them: *the starry heavens above me and the moral law within me.*

Taken by itself, this has a rather romantic tinge to it.

There is only so much one can fit on a gravestone, of course. If one reads a bit further on in Kant's second *Critique* (from which the quote comes), you will find that there is nothing romantic or heartening about the starry heavens. These heavens constitute 'an unbounded magnitude with worlds upon worlds and systems of systems':

> The view of a countless multitude of worlds an-
> nihilates, as it were, my importance as an *animal*
> *creature,* which after it has been for a short time
> provided with vital force (one knows not how)
> must give back to the planet (a mere speck in
> the universe) the matter from which it came.
> (*CPrR,* 5: 162)[4]

The starry heavens are like a great machine, teeming with forces, moving with iron patterns of causal determinism.

Causal determinism is the view that everything that happens, including everything that you or I want, think, do, or dream, is entirely predetermined by the laws of nature. Certainly, you just said what you did because you wanted to: but you wanting to wasn't something you could have done anything about.

The determinism of the starry heavens unfolds for us in all sorts of way: in our genes, in early childhood formation, maybe in an abusive parental relationship, and then in experiences of being bullied and excluded, leading into problems with loneliness and addiction. Or, the story may be a sunnier one: a happy enough childhood, school, university, a satisfying career and relationships. But, in any case, for good or ill, what happens to us and what we do are preordained.

Kant considers this to be a deeply problematic perspective, which threatens to 'annihilate' our sense of our significance. Somehow, Kant thinks, the autonomous *I* that I think I am – free, acting, myself – seems left out of it all.

In particular, Kant worries that it destroys our ability to think of ourselves as free and as moral. Morality and freedom, for Kant, are bound together: you can only be moral, or immoral, and so praised or blamed for your actions, if they are genuinely your own, and not determined by iron laws of determinism. We would at least like the dignity of making our own mistakes. So, you see, the 'starry heavens above me' and the 'moral law within me' present themselves initially as antagonists, as enemies to each other.

A lot of what Kant does in his mature philosophy is about sorting out this problem. He has to sort out the problem of the starry heavens in order to secure what he comes to think that freedom requires.

This is the trap, the escape room. And as such, the escape room can be summed up as one of the fundamental types of yearning:

> A yearning for freedom, given the way in which we may feel determined by our genetics, or by vast historical and political forces.

*

Next, I will feed you the four clues which, if properly combined, will lead to release, to freedom. These clues are four
principles of Kant's philosophy, which illuminate the main
lines of his thinking:

(i) The 'inner value' of the world is freedom, *and nothing
     else*. Freedom means: setting ends for yourself, with-
     out being impacted upon by anything external to
     you. Other things may be admirable, or impressive,
     but they lack this value.

(ii) Reason is a larger category than knowledge. There
     is far more that we can have rational beliefs about
     than we can know about. This means that Kant
     would not recognise the validity of a debate between
     faith and reason – because faith, religious belief, is
     entirely within the scope of reason, even though it
     goes beyond the bounds of knowledge. Knowledge,
     for Kant, involves absolute certainty. In a few areas,
     such as geometry and mathematics, such certain-
     ty is possible. But where it is not, I can still have
     rational belief. I rationally believe, on the basis of
     weather forecasts and experience, that it won't rain
     this week, but I cannot know this. I rationally be-
     lieve that I can trust you to keep a promise, but I
     cannot know this.

(iii) Thinking about the 'conditions of possibility' for
     something can expand your knowledge, and your set
     of rational beliefs. Consider: if you know something,

or have a rational belief about something, you can then ask, 'What else must be true, or what else do I need to believe, in order to make this possible?' You then have warrant for affirming, for 'holding-for-true', whatever comes out of this conceptual investigation. You might not *know* it, but, as we have seen from the second principle, knowledge is not everything. There is a caveat here: anything you come up with must not contradict something that you know. But that is a fairly minimal test, precisely because we do not know very much.

(iv) Kant thinks in a way that is big and binary. His philosophy tends to lead us to a crossroads, where he finds that *everything* (created and uncreated, the world and God) is either *this way* or *that way*, where what is offered is an entire package, a whole and encompassing worldview. In relation to the question of morality and freedom the options are these: we either live in a 'moral world' where freedom is possible, or we live in a world of mechanistic determinism, where freedom and morality are impossible. The former world has value, the latter world is a 'mere desert', entirely without value.

Together, these four principles go to the heart of the Kantian challenge to God-talk, set out earlier, effectively undoing it. Kant does not say that to have a *rational belief*, you need to have a combination of concepts and experience. What he says is that to have *knowledge*, you need something like this combination.

Furthermore, it is essential, Kant thinks, for human life and flourishing, that we have lots of rational beliefs that are not knowledge.

If you only permitted yourself beliefs that had the absolute certainty of knowledge, you probably wouldn't get up in the morning. You certainly wouldn't do very much with your day, or with other people, about whom you technically 'know' nothing. It would be very difficult to form trusting, and risk-taking, relationships.

Kant is also willing, determined even, to think in ambitious terms: about whole ways in which the world is. He finds himself able to make pronouncements about this that go far beyond anything we can empirically observe, but without going beyond what he thinks reason can warrant.

*

So, how does Kant release himself from the escape room?

He does this by developing a position that has the rather forbidding name 'transcendental idealism'. I'll come back in a few minutes to why he calls it this.

It will be easier to understand this if we know what the position is.

Kant's answer is this: at a fundamental level of our existence, so fundamental that we can never directly experience it, we are each of us non-spatial and non-temporal. This is where our freedom and our moral struggle *really* happens: in a non-spatial and non-temporal realm, of which our temporal biographies are in some sense appearances.

Putting it briskly, the reasoning goes as follows: if space and time are features of the world in itself, and directly created by God, they go 'all the way down' into reality, and we are contained within them. This, in philosophical terms, would be realism, not idealism: space and time are real, whatever our ideas are about space and time. This is bad news for freedom because, Kant believes, space and time are through and through deterministic in ways described by Newtonian mechanism.

If, then, space and time are features of our reception of the world, and not of the world in itself, this is good news for the possibility of freedom. This, in philosophical terms, is 'idealism': space and time are only real insofar as we have certain ideas. Such idealism about space and time enables us to believe in freedom and morality. There is a conceptual possibility that fundamental reality could be quite other than it appears to be. Here we can recall the third principle: something providing the 'conditions of possibility' of something is itself permitted to provide warrant for a belief, as long as it does not contradict what we know, because reason is a larger category than knowledge (the second principle).

Kant uses a number of terms to describe the spatial-temporal world that we experience:

The empirical realm.
The sensible realm.
The phenomenal realm ('phenomenon' comes from the Greek term that means 'that which appears').

Characteristically – recall principle three – Kant looks for the 'conditions of possibility' of the empirical realm.

One of the terms Kant uses to describe the 'conditions of possibility' is 'transcendental'. If a principle is transcendental, it means that it provides the 'conditions of possibility' of something else.

Why does he use this term?

Probably because *transcendere* in Latin means 'that which goes beyond': the conditions of possibility go beyond, or stand behind, other things.

Kant also uses a number of terms to describe the world as it is in itself, prior to and independent of our reception of it, and our filtering of it. These terms include:

The noumenal realm.
The intelligible realm.
The supersensible realm.

For Kant, the 'noumenal realm' is the fundamental ground of the world of appearances, whereby 'noumenal objects' impact upon us.

These noumenal objects, things as they are in themselves, bring about our experience, which experience is always filtered through the ways in which we receive the world. This experience is spatial and temporal.

Things-in-themselves, though, are not spatial or temporal. Space and time arise from our way of receiving the world.

Hence, we could ask:

> What are the conditions of possibility of the world as it appears to us?

If space and time were really things-in-themselves, this would be realism, and hence a 'transcendental realism' about space and time.

If space and time are features of how we receive the world, this would be idealism, and hence a 'transcendental idealism' about space and time.

Kant is a transcendental idealist about space and time.

Although we understand that all our experience is always on this side of this mediation, coming downstream of how we receive the world, we also understand that it is dependent upon the world as it is in itself, even though we cannot know anything much about this world, except that it does indeed ground our experience.

*

I'll step back here and offer an analogy, which may help to illustrate what Kant's transcendental idealism is, and is not, saying.[5]

Imagine you are watching a football match on TV, and that it is in black-and-white (unlikely, I know, but go with me, for the sake of the analogy). Is the game you are watching the 'game-in-itself'? Well, no: you *know* that there is a real game happening somewhere, which has quite different qualities. The game-in-itself is in three dimensions, and it is in colour, for example. The game on the screen is in two dimensions, and in black-and-white.

So, does the game-on-the-screen have anything to do with the game-in-itself?

Of course: you know that the game-on-the-screen only exists, and is only unfurling the way it is, *because* of the way the game-in-itself is proceeding. When the pixels that represent the attacking Newcastle United midfielder move swiftly through the central channels, and then appear to evade the opposition defender, this is because something has happened to the real body and person of the midfielder. The game-on-the-screen is a true, but partial, appearance of the game-in-itself. It is not remote from, or unrelated to, the game-in-itself. But you do know that the game-in-itself is not in two dimensions, and is not in black-and-white.

The situation is similar, for Kant, with space and time: these are like the two-dimensional black-and-whiteness of the screened game. You *know*, if you are Kant, that these are features of how the world appears to us, and not of how the world truly is. This means you know that the world is not causally determined as it appears. Freedom and morality are possible. But, as with the game-on-the-screen, this does not mean that everything that appears in space and time is an illusion, or that it has nothing to do with the world-in-itself. Like the pixels representing the midfielder, everything that unfolds in space and time only does so because of what happens in the world-in-itself. The only difference is that we can never buy a ticket to see the match in person: the world-in-itself will always be off-limits to us.

This is probably the place to stop the analogy. It is tempting to push on, and to say that the referee in the game-in-itself plays the role of something like God in Kant's philosophy: of ensuring that virtue is rewarded with happiness, and that the right team wins.

But that, of course, is not what happens.

As every football fan knows, referees always support the opposing team, and rob us of what belongs to us.

Kant would say: God will be their judge, and return the stolen points, and make it that we won the league.

There you are. Another problem, to which God could be the answer.

Referees.

*

'Transcendental idealism', in the interpretation that I have offered here, has three dimensions.

First of all, it sets the limits to knowledge, which, as we have seen, is a more constrained category than reason.

Secondly, within those limits, knowledge is made secure.

Thirdly, it opens up possibilities for rational thinking and believing beyond the limits of knowledge.

That is to say, transcendental idealism retains a type of humility about what we can know, while opening up the possibility that the way things are is fundamentally different from the way things appear to be. Things appear to be determined, but this is just an appearance. We can believe in freedom without irresponsibility.

*

Human beings, you, I, everyone, appear in space and time: that is where we seem to have our life.

Everything that Kant says about things in space and time being appearances of something more fundamental is, therefore, true about us also.

This leads to some fairly dizzying implications.

For Kant, the entire history of human actions, as with everything that appears, is the appearance of that which is fundamentally non-spatial and non-temporal.

This position can be understood as delivered by a combination of the four principles set out above.

Kant asks, 'what sort of *entire world* is the condition of possibility of the freedom that is the inner-value of the world?' (principle four). Transcendental idealism is part of Kant's answer. Because it does not contradict what we know, but only goes beyond it, it is rational to believe it (principle two). Because, Kant thinks, it is the *only entire world*, the only way the world can be, that can sustain such an ambitious conception of freedom (principle one), we should believe in it (principle three). Furthermore, it is not rational to believe more than is required in order to sustain the possibility of the freedom that is the inner value of the world. In these two constraints ('we should believe' and 'believe no more than is required') lie Kant's discipline and humility.

*

With this in place, we are able to understand Kant's conception of freedom. The possibility of freedom is *itself* the great religious hope of Kant's whole system. Only if there is a dimension of reality beyond deterministic mechanism, is end-setting, and so freedom, possible. The alternative to a world with freedom is a universe without end-setting, and without freedom, which Kant tells us repeatedly, would be a sort of 'desert' with no 'inner value'.

Believing in the possibility of freedom already, and in itself, leans into what we might call religious hope: the hope that things are not as they seem, and that there is a dimension to reality which is saturated with reason (acting for ends), wherein which we find our 'proper selves'. The result of a fully free 'Kingdom of Ends', as Kant puts it, where everyone acts harmoniously and universally, would be 'happiness' where 'everything goes according to the wish and will' of every 'rational being in the world' (*CPrR*, 5:124).

Kant then has two different ways in which he uses the concept of God. One of these ways I find more coherent with his overall picture than the other, but they are both present in his texts.

The first way involves thinking of God as a first among equals in the 'Kingdom of Ends': like our proper selves, God is beyond and outside of space and time, in the realm of freedom. God is a being in this realm with superior attributes.

The second way involves regarding the whole concept of reason, and the realm of freedom, as itself divine, because it brings about a fundamental reconciliation and harmonisation between all rational beings, and because it overcomes, finally, the problem of evil and suffering in the realm of appearances.

The second conception seems to me more compatible with the overall drift of Kant's conception, and it seems to be the position that he moves towards in the final years of his life. The problem with the first conception – God as another being, a first amongst equals – is that there is nothing much that another being, albeit a powerful one, can do for us, given that we must achieve everything through our own unfettered and unassisted freedom.

But when we ourselves grow into the full space of freedom and reason, we become, for Kant, like God: replete with harmony, happiness, reason and order.

*

About this way of thinking, I have a few thoughts.

First of all, I have to admit that some people find Kant's thought, or, at least, something in my presentation of it, baffling to the point of irritation. You may be such a person. It can even make people angry, a bit like the way in which I can become frustrated by sympathetic pushers of Spinoza. And come to think of it, Spinozists are nearly always frustrated by Kant.

The reactions I've received about Kant include:

It's all so weird.
It's spooky and disembodied.

There is such a split in the thinking, between how things are, and how they appear.

So, is everything I experience an illusion?

It has nothing to do with ordinary life.

Again, the emotion in the reactions is interesting, when reflecting on the way in which argument manifests a worldview, turns it around, displays it, shows how it moves and reacts. When you've seen enough of a worldview or philosophy moving under pressure, it helps you to know if this is something you want to dance with or not. The reaction, as with dance partners, is pretty visceral, coming from diverse parts of the self. Whether you find the position attractive, repulsive or just bizarre, won't simply be determined by the validity or otherwise of the abstract moves in an argument.

My visceral reaction to *this* Kant, and these Kantian patterns of thought, is one of deep attraction and fascination, which doesn't mean I'm persuaded or 'agree' with the philosophy.

But I'm drawn in. I say more about this personally in chapter 12 ('Is It Over?'), but I can say something at a more general level here.

The Kant that I found, when I read him properly, is so much more lively, dynamic, exciting and full of a type of yearning for happiness, than the rather dreary Kant I was first exposed to.

This Kant throws a rather psychedelic light on a lot of 'Western' assumptions about individualism and freedom.

As we've seen, Kant's notion of freedom and of individual dignity is frequently asserted to be one of the cornerstones of Western values, undergirding UN charters, and assumptions in jurisprudence and medical ethics.

How intriguing to think that the undergirding idea goes deep into a realm beyond space and time.

We might repeat here the Iris Murdoch passage about the ideal Kantian subject:

> ...free, independent, lonely, powerful, rational, responsible, brave, the hero of so many novels and books of moral philosophy...the offspring of the age of science, confidently rational and yet increasingly aware of his alienation from the material universe which his discoveries reveal.[6]

And then reflect that, for Kant, everything that occurs in our empirical biography, including our interior lives (which would feature dreaming and imagination) is an unfurling, in space and time, of something that lies beyond it.

'As a human being', Kant writes, a person is 'only the appearance of himself' (GW, 4: 437). Our empirical selves are not unrelated to our noumenal selves, our proper selves: they are the appearance in space and time, the moving image of eternity, of our true selves outside of space and time.

Kant's 'proper self' (*GW*, 4: 437) is the locus and source of true freedom: this self never directly and fully appears, yet is the generative source of everything that does appear across the stretch of our psychic lives.

This is hugely significant.

Kant is telling us that the subject who enjoys true freedom is never our empirical self, or the self of our empirical ego-biographies. It is not a striving and conscious heroic individual. It is the whole, entire, true, proper self, which remains unknown to us, but is the source of what we know of as 'us'.

*

I'm not entirely sure what one does with all this, except perhaps to marvel at how we managed to make such an intriguing and spiritually exotic creature – Immanuel Kant with his dreams of divinity and freedom – so dreary and dismal.

Although she is not writing, at all, about Kant, I find that some words of the twentieth-century American poet and essayist Elizabeth Bishop somehow precisely evoke for me something of the atmosphere of Kant. Bishop writes:

> Perhaps we shall never know the companion in
> ourselves who is with us all our lives, the nearness
> of our minds at all times to the rare person whose

> heart quickens when a bird climbs high and alone
> in the clear air.

I find this a striking evocation of something like Kant's 'proper self': the free, whole, entire and original source of all our thoughts and actions, disclosed but veiled in each moment of our empirical biographies, which pass for us like the moving images of our own eternity, which eternity happens not somewhere else, remote from us, but in an inaccessible nearness. As Bishop puts it, in a 'quiet hour', the 'mind finds its Sea, the wide, quiet plane with different lights in the sky and different, more secret sounds'.[7]

8

Enchanting

How to be at home in the universe (and be an atheist).

You may think that things are going a bit too well, in this book, for belief in God.

Throughout, I've been eager to show that belief in God is not stupid or ignorant, and to argue that there are more textures and nuances in belief than are widely known about.

You might put this together with my confession early on in the book:

I came out religious it seems.

It might all begin to feel like a bit of a stitch-up.

In my defence I might suggest that in some parts of the wider culture, it is articulate but unnuanced atheists such as Ricky Gervais and Richard Dawkins who have made the most noise.

Nonetheless, at the same time, within some circles, I also think that unbelief and atheism do not get their fair dues.

In particular, this happens in some theological circles, and amongst those philosophers who do believe in God.

There is a pattern of thinking which goes a bit like this:

> To give an adequate account of human life – its meaning, our yearnings and aspirations – you need to be able to speak about realities such as goodness, beauty, freedom, hope and a sense of transcendence.
>
> Religious philosophies are able to give such an account.
>
> Atheistic philosophies have poor resources to draw on: they focus on matter in motion, the laws of science and mathematics, and human desires, which are understood as sheer impulses.
>
> If it is true that we do not know whether or not there is a God, what we are thrown back on is the importance of offering an adequate account of our lives. Religious philosophy is able to address important dimensions of existence that atheistic philosophy does not.
>
> Therefore, given that we don't have proof in this area, religious philosophy is proved to be superior.

The problem with this line of argument, it seems to me, is that it critiques only the crudest forms of atheist philosophy.

It is a principle of fairness that you should match like with like: the best atheist philosophy with the best religious philosophy, not the best religious philosophy with the worst atheist philosophy. The worst atheist philosophy is, appropriately enough, produced by figures who have no formal training in philosophy at all, such as Richard Dawkins.

If we really want to think about atheism, and the levels of humanity and self-transcendence that atheist philosophy can be capable of, we need to look at higher-grade atheistic philosophy.

One of the most stimulating contemporary philosophers I know of, working in this area, is the Indian philosopher Akeel Bilgrami. Bilgrami is a professor at Columbia University, a self-identifying atheist who was raised a Muslim, and who writes with great sensitivity about Gandhi's philosophy, including what Gandhi says about the sacred.

If we want exposure to subtle and insightful atheism, we could do worse, I suggest, than look at what Bilgrami has to say about enchantment.

*

The idea of enchantment has taken a sort of hold on many people.

At an arts, literature and music festival held in the south of England in June 2023, there is a whole programme dedicated to enchantment. A wooded area is called the 'en-chanted zone'.

It is charming.

Ribbons, bells and wind-chimes are tied to the branches of trees. There are fairy lights wrapped around and between the trunks of the trees. The paths have been strewn with gold-painted wooden chips so that they sparkle and glisten. Music is playing softly from hidden speakers: an ethereal flute and a Celtic harp.

The wood is always busy, and the people in it look happy and, well…enchanted.

Lots of people want enchantment, and many of them would like this without having to believe, as they might think of it, crazy shit, and without having to swallow a whole load of dogma.

*

Akeel Bilgrami reaches for an 'enchanted' account of nature. Such an account envisages nature as containing 'properties of value and meaning'. Strikingly, Bilgrami wants to distance this re-enchantment from any approach that identifies the source of nature's value in 'anything sacral'. Bilgrami does not want to draw on the idea of God or the divine.

What this means is this: it isn't just that you find nature beautiful, and that you enjoy it. Nature *is* beautiful. Just as you might consider that people have rights and entitlements to be treated in certain ways, so also does nature: the river may be said to have rights, because of a value that is intrinsic to it.

So, for example, one group of people hold a funeral for a melting glacier.

Only if we embrace such an enchanted account of nature, Bilgrami thinks, will it be possible to enjoy what he calls an unalienated relationship with the world. The problem with an unenchanted conception of nature is that it treats the world simply as a resource to be exploited. The ecological consequences of this attitude are all too obvious now.

The idea of the 'unalienated life' already has some religious undertones. Bilgrami explains the notion of the 'unalienated life' in terms of being 'at home in the world', which is one of the core 'yearnings' I identified in chapter 2 at work in generating belief in God.

Bilgrami finds 'being at home in the world' to be 'an apt expression':

> [P]artly because it leaves things at a high level of generality and is able to accommodate a wide range of belonging. The term 'world' in that expression is used in [a] highly general sense...It includes both the natural world and the social world but in an integrated way, not as two separate worlds.[1]

Bilgrami admits that for Gandhi, the notion of an unalienated life is inextricably bound up with his belief in God and his devotion to the 'idea of a sacralized nature'. As an 'atheist', which Bilgrami 'confesses to being', he finds that the 'deeper point that underlies' Gandhi's concept of 'an un-alienated relation' can be construed in terms of 'value rather than sacralization'.[2]

Nothing can block Bilgrami's translation of the language of the sacral into that of value.

Nonetheless, we might wonder about the assumption that the positing of value needs to be the 'deeper point' that we should take from Gandhi.

Why is the deeper point not an insight into the true role played – beyond any suspected superstition and pre-Enlightenment mythology – in the thought of Gandhi, and others, by the notion of the divine? We could talk about two different 'lexical fields', which is to say, a range of language associated with one, or another, way of talking. One lexical field involves the language of values, rights and duties. Another lexical field contains terms such as divine, sacred, holy. Why is one lexical field (values) assumed to be 'more fundamental'? For Gandhi, it is the lexical field of the divine that is more fundamental. For Bilgrami, the fundamental lexical field is the one that speaks of values.

I can imagine at this point some theologians pushing a few difficult questions:

How can an atheist philosopher ground the notion that the world has intrinsic value, even if there is nothing sacred about it?

Where does such value come from?

And how can we perceive it?

Bilgrami has answers to these questions.

*

To understand Bilgrami's position, we need to attend to his distinction between what he calls internalist and externalist conceptions of value. I'll explain what this means.

You are an 'internalist' about value if you think that value is something that *we* generate with our 'tendencies, desires and moral sentiments',[3] which we then 'project' upon the world.

Answer the following question:

> Is value (goodness, for example) out there in the
> world, independently of human beings?

If you say 'no', you are probably an internalist about values. If you say 'yes', you are closer to the 'externalist' point of view.

As Bilgrami puts it, one is an 'externalist' about value if one considers that 'the world, the perceptible world we inhabit, over and above containing the properties that natural science studies, contains value properties (or more simply values) that we perceive as making normative demands on us to which our practical agency responds'.[4]

The notion of being 'normative' involves the notion of *should*: normative demands are demands that we *ought* to attend to, in contrast, say, to obnoxious or irrelevant demands, which we are permitted to ignore or refuse.

A particular contribution from Bilgrami is to link such externalism about value to the notion of being an agent, a free actor in the world. To show this link takes a bit of unpacking.

The place to begin is by considering the following question:

> When someone asks us, 'Do you desire *x*?', are
> we prompted to ponder our own minds or are
> we prompted to consider whether *x* is desirable?

Let's offer a few examples:

I ask: 'Do you think it is raining?'

What do you do?

Do you undertake a sort of inventory of all your thoughts, to see if you think it is raining? What thoughts and beliefs are there in my head? Can I find the 'belief that it is raining' somewhere in here?

Or, do you just look out of the window?

Hopefully, you just look out of the window. Why do you do this? Well, because you are an 'externalist' about whether it is raining or not. Rain is out there in the world, or it isn't. It isn't primarily and originally a belief that is in you, which you then project upon the world. You can check whether it's raining – you just need to look outside.

I say: 'Do you think peace and justice is desirable? or 'Do you think it is desirable to avoid running over this dog?'

What do you do?

Do you do the inner inventory of thoughts and desires, to see if you do in fact have the desire not to run over the dog, or to endorse peace and justice? If you carry out this inventory, and find that there is no such desire, would you then declare 'it is not desirable, because I find I have no desire here'?

Or do you accept that peace and justice are desirable regardless of how you or anyone else feels about it at any particular moment? When you are faced with a dog, do you simply swerve, just like you would look out of the window to check whether it's raining?

I'd feel a lot safer around you if, in both cases, you give the second answer: you just look and see whether it is desirable, because the values of peace and justice, and not running over dogs, are just *there* externally in the world.

Bilgrami also suggests that it will be much better for *you* also to think in the second way. This is where the connection with being a free agent in the world comes in.

The wrong response, to the raining question, or the dog on the driveway, was to think that our job is to 'step back and consider' the question 'by scanning our minds'. In the rain case, we scan our minds for beliefs; in the dog case, we scan our minds to check for our desires. In both cases, we should not scan our beliefs or desires, but simply look and see: is it raining? Is this desirable?

Consider how odd the mind-scanning perspective on ourselves is. We are regarding ourselves as an object of detached observation, an object of study and research:

> Does this human being have this desire or belief?

With no mention that this human being is I, me, myself, it is as if we are looking at a third person, the human being with whom I happen to share a name and birthday. As Bilgrami puts it, this suggests 'that our desires were presented to us in a way that was accessible to us only when our angle on ourselves was…in the *third* person.'[5] I almost cease to exist as a proper agent and actor in the world, seeking the good, and avoiding or resisting the bad. I'm just constantly observing the contents of the mind of the person to whom I happen to be identical. I am no longer an agent, inside of my own freedom. Instead, I put on a white coat and observe myself.

*

> Do you love me? Am I lovable?

I don't know. Let me go and check my neural circuits, and the structure of my beliefs and desires. I'll get back to you.

Don't bother. I have my answer already. You had one thought too many there.

*

Value and enchantment are *really there* in the world, although our ability to detect them is tied up with the capacities and endowments that we have, given the sort of beings that we are. We move about, as free and limited agents, responding to this structured and dense world of value and disvalue.

The notion of the 'unalienated life' is bound up, therefore, with Bilgrami's commitment to an enchanted world, where we take an 'externalist' view on values. Living such a life involves 'being sensitive to – and thus aptly responsive to – the demands made on us by the value or disvalue that we perceive in the world we inhabit':

> If one sees the world (including nature) as containing values and disvalues rather than merely containing what the natural sciences study, one way to conceive of being at home in the world is to see oneself as being attuned in one's responses to what those value properties we perceive demand of us.[6]

Bilgrami's philosophy does seem, to me, to re-enchant the world with many things that religious people yearn for.

Why does Bilgrami so resolutely avoid the language of the sacred, even though he is not, himself, hostile to religion or religious belief? It is no part of Bilgrami's project, for example, to persuade people not to be religious, or not to believe. He likes religious people and finds religious belief often to be a force for good, for unalienated living.

I'm going to offer two different interpretations of why someone who adopts Bilgrami's position might avoid the concept of God. Both, or neither, might have some purchase, for some people. Again, we witness the variety of forms of belief and unbelief.

*

One interpretation might be this: whether or not you speak about God depends on how hopeful your notion of enchantment really is, and how consoling. If it turns out that re-enchantment is not that consoling or hopeful for Bilgrami, this might account for why he embraces Gandhi's category of value, whilst letting go of the sacred.

Consider: when the concept of the 'unalienated life' is employed, it sets off certain taste buds. We expect to be led into a lexical field of other concepts, which include categories such as being fulfilled, or living a happy, rounded and balanced life. We want at least some equivalent to ribbons, bells and fairy lights.

But when we properly attend to Bilgrami's account of the unalienated life, we see that this is not what we are being offered. The vital element of the unalienated life is a correct perception of the moral values and disvalues in the world. It might be that we live in a perfectly awful world: full of threat and impending disaster, and shot through with disvalue. As long as you *see* this aptly and correctly, you are living the unalienated life. As Bilgrami puts it at one point, 'to see the world aright and to overcome alienation are not two things, but one and the same'.[7]

There is, here, a possible explanation for why we would not use the language of divinity. Perhaps one is only inclined to use the concept of divinity to describe the same facts pointed to by Bilgrami, where we have the hope that some of our more optimistic taste buds are satisfied.

If we use the concept of God/the divine, this means that we may expect some consolation, hope, peace or promise, at least to some degree, even if this unfolds in a way that is bracing, and that involves a level of personal sacrifice, and even if the 'consolation' may not be a consolation that is particular *to me*.

Bilgrami's notion of the unalienated life has more to do with a correct perception of reality than with any sort of happiness, peace or consolation. There is no expected positive emotion or result from the unalienated perception of value and disvalue, for me, or for anyone else.

I was fortunate enough to be able to put this suggestion to Bilgrami in a conversation.

He said that it was an interesting account of why he did not reach for the concept of the divine and the sacred, but added:

[T]hese are your words, your ideas, not mine.

*

On reflection, I'm less convinced by the interpretation just offered.

As we've seen with Stoicism and Spinoza, plenty of religious belief is actually quite resigned and pessimistic, especially about this world, or how things will go for you personally.

Also, there is more hope around in Bilgrami's picture than the comments above suggest, about which more in a minute.

This leads me to an alternative interpretation, and a counterproposal to the suggestion made above, that enchantment and hope might lead us to believe in God.

The counterproposal is this: that the motivation to reach out towards the divine could be lessened, insofar as the world, of which we are a part, is *not* so denuded of enchantment. In the terms set out earlier in the chapter, if we embrace a more 'externalist' view of value, we may not be so starved of the value we need, and so, perhaps, we won't make such fanciful leaps as believing in God.

Maybe that is how it is, for some people, in any case.

*

This brings me to the undoubted element of hope in Bilgrami's philosophy.

Bilgrami affirms the positive effects of an unalienated perception of the world: seeing the world aright 'enlarges us', it 'improves us'. It is good for us to see the world aright.

This makes sense within Bilgrami's wider picture. When we look out upon the world, we see a world that is structured with values and disvalues. It would be odd if, when looking at other human beings and ourselves, *we* were the exception. We would expect there to be real goods for us, real flourishing and harm.

When we perceive ourselves aright, we must also perceive beings structured with values, goods and disvalues.

After all, we are part of the enchanted world.

9

No Greater Than

How to have it all (and be a Christian).

The outstanding feature of Christianity, for me – why I like it so much – is that it is greedy.

Where Stoicism, Spinozism and Kantianism all tell us to trim our desires to some degree, Christianity, or the tradition within it that grips me, opens up like a flower reaching towards the sun when it comes to a desire for life, for vitality, for healing and for love.

The prominent atheist Bertrand Russell wrote an essay, 'Why I am not a Christian'. If I had to put on a postcard why I am one, I would scribble phrases such as the following:

Open the gates.
That's not enough.
Still not enough.
I need more.
Undo me.
Fulfil me.
I want to be unhinged.

I know that this might come as a surprise to some readers, whose encounter with Christianity might lead them to expect a buttoned-up and guilt-driven suppression of vitality and life. This experience of Christianity might be direct or indirect, through painful experience, or through prejudice and anecdote.

I don't deny the reality of these experiences. The pervasiveness of such experiences and prejudices gives us all the more reason to explore a less buttoned-up strand of Christianity, running through thinkers such as St Anselm of Canterbury and St Thomas Aquinas.

Just as the best counter to the Kantian challenge was Kant himself, so the best response to the repression of life and vitality in the name of Christianity might be Christianity itself.

*

I'm going to begin by asking what sort of word the word 'God' is.

Is it, for example, a name (like 'Richard'), or a title (like 'king')?

Well, it doesn't seem that 'God' functions like a name or a title. Names and titles seem to be too contingently related to their objects. That is to say, the name/title and the object can too easily fall apart and be separated. They need not have been attached in the way that they are.

The paradigmatic use of names is along the following lines:

This individual is called Richard.

And a typical ascription of a title would be along these lines:

Richard is the king/pope.

In both cases, Richard might have gone by a different name, or not have been king/pope (and one day will not be). It would be odd to say:

This individual is called God.

Or

This individual has the title of God.

The identification is too contingent and dependent upon a type of baptism or dubbing.

To be *God*, within classical monotheism, we seem to need a stronger connection between God and what makes God God.

I knew a young child (not my own, for the record) who seriously believed, at the age of six, that he was God. His concerned atheist parents – friends of ours – asked me, as a philosophical theologian, to talk with him about this. He insisted that he had made, for example, the beach and sea in front of us, 'before I was born', he explained, astutely cutting off a potentially awkward line of questioning. For the record, the child, now a teenager, is doing fine. He has, wisely, dropped his claims to divinity, or, at least, prudently, stopped talking about them.

I had some sympathy with the child.

I confess that as a young child I did sometimes find myself wondering why *I* wasn't God (I knew that I wasn't), just as I also wondered why *I* had not been born into the title of being the Prince of Wales. This sort of confusion is only possible when we think of the word 'God' as being like a title.

As children grow into the language, they find out that this is not a correct use of the concept. Believers may use titles to evoke various properties of God, and what is owed to God ('king', 'father' and 'lord'), but it does not seem that the concept 'God' is a title.

*

Even if the word 'God' does not seem to work like a name, there is an interesting feature of names that might be relevant when talking about God.

Think about the way in which we can accurately point to someone, using their name, without having much in the way of descriptive knowledge about them, or, even, with a false description.

I point across the room, and I say:

> Peter is drinking a martini.

In fact, Peter is drinking water, but nobody would say that I've failed to point to Peter.

In other cases, we can build upon the sheer act of pointing, and augment this with some limited and minimal descriptive information.

Imagine that I am walking across a crowded room, and I overhear a colleague saying the sentence:

> Barbara Tuchman was a significant twentieth-century historian.

Before this, say, I had never heard of Barbara Tuchman, but I can now use this knowledge in conversation. In the opposite corner of the room, I join a group in conversation. One of the group points to a portrait of Barbara Tuchman and asks me, 'Who was Barbara Tuchman?' Immediately, I can offer some information to my conversation partner, building upon our shared ability to refer to the same person: 'Oh, she was an important historian.'

I said above that the word 'God' does not seem to be a name, because names are only contingently connected to the individuals who bear them.

But, there is another category of language use, called 'natural kind' terms. These terms pick out kinds of things that we think are 'natural', out there in the world, whatever we think about them. Natural kind terms include concepts such as:

Water
Gold
Lemon
Dog
Cat
Tiger

As with names, we can accurately point to gold and tigers, without full or accurate descriptions of these realities.

Maybe I think tigers have claws made of quartz crystal. I'm wrong about this, but I could still correctly identify a tiger.

When we learn to speak, our ability to refer to things such as 'lemons', 'tigers' or 'cats' far exceeds our ability to give accurate descriptive accounts of these things.

Philosophers have been interested in the way in which this ability to refer to things without much knowledge about them is essential, in everyday life but also in the development of scientific theories.

We might consider, here, the way in which a term such as 'gene' is used by scientists. At first, we might not know much about it. Scientists begin with a pretty minimal account, such as:

> A 'gene' is whatever mechanism it is that is responsible for the inheritance of acquired characteristics.[1]

Our understanding of the 'gene' is constantly developing, in such a way that we enrich our descriptive accounts of it.

In the case of natural kind terms, we accurately point to things, whilst acknowledging considerable limitations on what can be known:

> The natural kind x is that, whatever it is, which does this *or* has these features.

This kind of device – a type of structured pointing without knowledge – can be used about other types of reality. Consider, for example, black holes:

> A black hole is that, whatever it is, which sucks in everything around it, including light.

What about the concept of 'God'?

*

Some recent theologians have found that the way in which names and natural kind terms work is helpful, when thinking about the word 'God'. Names and natural kind terms can point to something, even without knowing much about what they point to. But there is a shape to what they point to: it is *this*, whatever it is, which does *that*.

The element of 'unknowing' in the use of natural kind terms is significant here. We cannot directly *describe*, not fully – or sometimes, not at all – what we refer to.

This resonates with some theological instincts about the unknowability and indescribability of God. The theologian Janet Martin Soskice celebrates the 'agnosticism of our formulations' about God, when we use the concept to point without describing:

> [The] insight that we say nothing of God, but only point toward Him is the basis for the tentative and avowedly inadequate stammerings by which we attempt to speak of God and His acts.[2]

If we permit pointing without describing, it seems that we can block a familiar line of atheist attack. Consider, for example, this line of attack from the prominent mid-twentieth-century atheist, A. J. Ayer:

> To say that something transcends the human understanding is to say that it is unintelligible. And what is

unintelligible cannot be significantly described... If
one allows that it is impossible to define God in intelligible terms, then one is allowing that it is impossible
for a sentence both to be significant and to be about
God. If a mystic admits that the object of his vision
cannot be described, then he must also admit that he
is bound to talk nonsense when he describes it.[3]

But, now, if we are allowed to point without an accurate
description, it doesn't seem correct to say, as Ayer does, that
if we cannot define God, we shouldn't use this concept at all.

*

With natural kind terms, there is some sort of conceptual
content to the pointing. That is to say, there is an overall
context, with some shape to what we are looking for. In the
case of God, how might we fill in the gap in the following
statement?

God is that, whatever it is, that $[x, y, z]$.

In fact, the Christian tradition does offer up a rule for using
the word God, and pointing.

Anselm of Canterbury (1033–1109) was a theologian
and reluctant Archbishop of Canterbury. So vexed was

he in this role that he wrote to Eulalia, the Abbess of Shaftesbury:

> I am so harassed in the archbishopric that if it were possible to do so without guilt, would rather die than continue in it.[4]

In an early text, called the *Monologion*, Anselm offers an extended meditation of the nature of God. Anselm desires, though, something simpler: 'one argument', from which all the themes of the longer *Monologion* could arise. This simpler argument Anselm provides in his text called the *Proslogion*. This short text is highly revered and studied by theologians from a wide range of traditions. From my personal experience as a student and teacher in theology and religion departments, and interacting with a range of theologians and philosophers of religion, I'd say that this is one of the most highly esteemed texts in the Western Christian intellectual tradition.

Anselm had to carve out some time in his busy schedule to write it. It takes the form of a prayer, where he talks to God, whilst also addressing and admonishing himself:

> Come now, insignificant man, fly for a moment from your affairs, escape for a little while from the tumult of your thoughts. Put aside now your weighty cares

and leave your wearisome toils. Abandon yourself
for a little to God and rest for a little in Him...

Come then, Lord my God, teach my heart where
and how to seek You, where and how to find you...[5]

For Anselm, the 'single argument' arises from a type of
pointing into a conceptual space, whilst speaking the word
'God'.

Now we believe that You are something than which
nothing greater can be thought.[6]

How does this work?

God is that than which nothing greater can be
thought.

This is not a description, as one might describe a dog as a
four-legged canine mammal. It is, rather, an act of pointing,
and a rule for thinking, in a way that has affinities with natural kinds and names.

Think of something – anything.
If you can think of a way in which that thing
could be greater – more beautiful, more stable,
larger, stronger, kinder – well then, that thing
cannot be God.

> Because God is that than which nothing
> greater can be thought.

It works as a sort of blackballing rule: throwing out of consideration a range of realities which might be magnificent and imposing, but which are not such that nothing greater than them can be thought.

*

What is frequently taken from Anselm's *Proslogion*, and set out in textbooks, is his so-called 'ontological argument'. *Ontos*, in Greek, means 'being', so the ontological argument is an argument for the existence of God derived from an understanding of the way in which God is. Briskly speaking, this is how the argument works:

> God is that than which nothing greater can be
> thought.

Consider two candidates for this title:

(i) A being with God's attributes (all-powerful and all-knowing and perfectly good) who happens not to exist.

(ii) A being with God's attributes (all-powerful and all-knowing and perfectly good) who exists necessarily. This being doesn't just 'happen' to exist, as the universe might.

Is (i) that than which nothing greater can be conceived? *No*, because (ii) is greater.

Therefore, if the concept of God even makes sense, it must be that God exists.

A witty twentieth-century philosopher once said that everyone knows that the ontological argument doesn't work, but nobody knows why.

This is perhaps not quite correct. Some people think that it does work, and others think they know why it doesn't.

But the working of the *argument* is not my prime concern. As I've mentioned a few times, I don't think arguments often really work, if by 'working' we mean forcing our assent the way that a properly constructed geometrical proof might. Although it is a less common usage, people sometimes speak of the 'argument' of a story, or a plot, by which they mean the unfolding of a central theme or narrative.

The sense in which the *Proslogion* offers an 'argument' would seem closer to this usage than to a geometrical proof. The central theme of the text, its 'argument', is all about yearning:

I pray, O God, that I may know You and love You, so that I may rejoice in You.[7]

... Let the knowledge of you grow in me here, and there [in heaven] be made complete; let Your love grow in me here and there be made complete, so that here my joy may be great in hope, and there be complete in reality.[8]

... Oh he who will enjoy [God]...what will be his and what will not be his! Whatever he wishes will certainly be his and whatever he does not wish will not be his. In fact, all the goods of body and soul will be there such that 'neither eye has seen, nor ear heard, nor the heart of man conceived' [1 Cor. 2:90].[9]

... For what do you love, O my flesh, what do you desire, O my soul? There it is, there it is, whatever you love, whatever you desire.[10]

... O human heart, O needy heart, O heart experienced in suffering, indeed overwhelmed by suffering, how greatly would you rejoice if you abounded in [God]![11]

The *Proslogion* is all about the depths of the heart's desire for life and love. I see Anselm hitting his hands against false ceilings:

No – that is not enough. There is more. Always more.

The formal theological expression of Anselm's pattern of thought here is encapsulated in what is called the 'Doctrine of Divine Simplicity'.

Today, this doctrine is not widely known about outside of academic circles, but it was crucial to almost all pre-modern theology, and is still widely assented to amongst theologians today. Meditating a little on divine simplicity, as I will do now, can show why God is not merely a 'super person', or an anthropomorphic projection.

The doctrine is all about a yearning for the more that never fully comes.

The concept of divine simplicity is a little strange and counterintuitive. In a sense, it is supposed to be impossible to understand, or, at least, impossible to grasp in a direct and positive sense. It is more that one can understand what the doctrine is denying.

Let's begin.

*

Once upon a time, I, Chris Insole, did not exist. Quite soon, relatively speaking, I will no longer exist, or not, at least, in quite the same form.

Chris Insole and existence can come apart. They do not belong intrinsically together.

Am I God?

Well, let's check, using our rule. Am I such that no greater than me can be conceived?

No, for many reasons. There are many ways of being greater than me, of course, but one of them, for Anselm, is related to the possibility of Chris Insole and existence coming apart. Something, or someone, whose existence could never be separated from it, would be greater. Such a something would be such that it *had to exist*. Its existence is not separable from it.

It might seem a strange way of talking, but we could say that Chris Insole plus existence is a composite reality, because existence has to be added to Chris Insole, and it can be subtracted. If Chris Insole and existence were somehow identical, if they couldn't come apart, we might say that Chris Insole was 'non-composite', or, in the term used by the tradition, 'simple'.

God and God's existence are, in some sense, identical. This, really, is what Anselm means when setting out the so-called 'ontological argument'. It belongs to God's nature to exist necessarily, in a way that is not true for anything else. Anything else is composite, with respect to existence.

This is part of what is meant by the classical doctrine of 'divine simplicity'.

But only part.

There is more.

Christianity is greedy: there is always more.

*

Chris Insole is a human being. But there were human beings before Chris Insole existed, and there will be human beings after he ceases to exist. Being human is my nature, but Chris Insole and human nature are separable. Chris Insole plus being human is a composite reality.

This is another way in which Chris Insole is not such that no greater can be conceived. Imagine a reality which is such that its individuality is inseparable from its nature. Imagine the stability, the indestructability of such a reality: a stability beyond even harmony, because its nature is inseparable from the individuality. Such a being is God: God and the divine nature are identical. They cannot come apart.

*

Chris Insole is writing this book, or, by the time you are reading it, he has written this book. But Chris Insole and the act of writing the book can come apart. Chris Insole existed before writing the book. He might not have done it, and after the action of doing it, he continues to exist (I hope that turns out to be an accurate prediction, for a little while).

For God, this is not how it is. For God, and in God, every action taken by God is (somehow, mysteriously) identical with everything else that is true of God: identical with God's nature (being divine), which is identical with God's existence and with God's individuality.

*

Chris Insole is 177 cm tall. But Chris Insole and being 177 cm tall can come apart. He wasn't always this tall, but still existed. As, and if, I get older, I will probably shrink a bit, but I will still be Chris Insole. I have many other such properties: hair colour, the shape of my nose, personality traits, things I know, and so on.

All these can change, and might have been otherwise. There is an instability to me.

But, for God, there is no such instability. All God's properties are, somehow, simply identical with all God's other properties, and with God's actions, and with God's existence and nature.

This is 'divine simplicity'. Every pre-modern thinker who believes in God accepts and endorses divine simplicity. Divine simplicity, or something like it, is also accepted by Islamic and Jewish theologians.

It seems obvious to them that God cannot come apart in the way that everything that is not God can.

*

Hopefully you are beginning to get the idea.

Any feature of the reality that is God, God's properties, actions, being, nature, existence is strictly, in a way that we cannot fully understand, identical with every other feature of God's reality, properties, actions, being, nature, existence. And it is an *identity* that goes beyond 'being harmonious'.

For theologians such as Anselm and Aquinas, divine simplicity is at the heart of why God is mysterious to us. We, and everything we experience and know, is 'composite'. God is utterly unlike this, in a way that is staggeringly beautiful, stable, indestructible forever, satiating, fulfilling, safe beyond words and worlds.

God really is not like a big supernatural person.

God is utterly unlike us, or anything like us.

Only such a God will be enough, and we will never get enough of such a God: always there will be more and more, forever and ever.

This is quite greedy. Maybe, a bit unhinged.

10

Life

How to have better conversations about God.

You have probably heard of 'think tanks'.

These are groups of usually like-minded types, who style themselves as thinkers and intellectuals, who approach an aspect of the human condition: often politics or economics, sometimes religion or culture.

The late cultural theorist Lauren Berlant used to run, at the University of Chicago, what she called a 'feel tank', in contrast to a 'think tank'.

Berlant had a political perspective and focused on what she called objects of 'cruel optimism'. By this, Berlant had in mind ways in which dreams and fantasies, which are important to us, can also harm and imprison us. Berlant particularly had in her sights nationalistic nostalgia and ideology:

> [O]ur politics – and our personal relationships, our path to happiness, are all fogged in by feelings we mostly misread. Our stumbling blocks are past attachments to fantasy and false hopes. Recovery, if it comes, is in saying goodbye, and moving on.[1]

I am not so committed, always, to letting go and moving on. Some things we may want to hold on to, or embrace in a new way, more tender, more committed, but less brittle.

But I like the provocative thought of a feel tank. Such a tank is not a place, but an event, that can be inaugurated whenever we talk and think feelingly.

Think tanks often end up being quite doctrinaire: they can have a particular ideology or political edge (right or left wing) to promulgate, sharpen and defend. At their worst, they become staffed by rather swivel-eyed types.

One would hope that a feel tank will take us in an opposite direction: towards greater variety, curiosity, a lack of dogma and certainty about ourselves and others. A feel tank should be staffed by wide-eyed and self-questioning types.

We do not *always* have to inhabit the feel tank, but sometimes, it might be a good idea. It might help us to be freer, and kinder. Anyway, we can try.

*

We began the book with a certain scepticism about what could be achieved when arguing about the existence and nature of God or the divine. I do not think it is possible to arrive at knowledge, or anything approaching certainty. I do not find that a certain style of argument in this area will ever be that persuasive. Arguments rarely convince someone to move from their position, whether that be theism, atheism or agnosticism.

Given this, I suggested we approach other ways of exploring the question of 'what is really going on, for and between you and me?', when the question of God is raised. The question was put in this way so as to involve us, personally and experientially, in the question. The question was also put in this way to flag up the aspiration to have better conversations, better disagreements, more empathy, compassion and freedom in thinking.

*

If we are not primarily searching for knowledge, or certainty, what are we doing when we discuss belief or unbelief in God, in a philosophical context?

I suggested that we were leaning into a constant feature of philosophy: the search for the wisdom that comes from self-knowledge, and the empathic understanding of others, and the differences and affinities between ourselves and others.

In other areas of intellectual life, where knowledge or certainty is more achievable, our goals might be different. But, with God, reason must accept some humility. There is a degree of non-coercive freedom, when it comes to speaking about God, or not speaking about God.

In this area, therefore, it may be appropriate to draw on your personal experience, commitments and involvements.

Personal experience, your own and that of others, can be evidence. It will, therefore, sometimes be appropriate to speak in the first person: 'I experienced this', 'I find this to be the case', and the second person, 'do you think this?', 'how does this sound to you?'.

This is especially so, given that religious belief or unbelief is so tied up with so many aspects of our human life: bodily and emotional, as well as intellectual and spiritual.

*

We have, then, filled out an approach to the question of belief or unbelief in God. We want an approach that is widely attentive to many facets of life. We want to be open to truth, but not dogmatic. We want to be curious, but not intrusive.

We have found there to be a lack of transparency, on the surface of the argument, about what is really going on when people are drawn or repelled by the idea of God.

What next?

Well, when there is a lack of transparency, we might investigate the reasons for it.

*

William James talks about the 'prestige bias' we have towards conscious and explicit rationalisations, and towards considerations which make us look good, or good enough.

Such conscious rationalisations are indispensable and vital.

But this shouldn't obscure the insight that most of our mental life does not occur at this level: most of it is much more chaotic and uncensored, with thoughts and feelings – some intrusive and unwelcome – erupting from our unconscious, where previous unforgotten memories suddenly erupt into consciousness, sometimes replete with emotion.

We do not fully understand ourselves. You only have to think about the overreaction at work, the unexpected offence taken at a friend's comments, or the obsession with a particular idea or person, whether wanted or not.

*

When the comedian Ricky Gervais takes a comic swing at belief in God, there can be something primitive about the audience reaction. I hear a type of savage relief and relish in the laughter, which goes beyond amusement.

I also hear, I fancy, a type of distress and anxiety, along with some relief and enjoyment at the release: a thrill that God, and those gullible religious believers, are getting a good kicking. Getting what's coming to them.

Others in the audience may squirm, or feel alienated, either out of consideration for believers whom they love, or out of a deep offence at being so attacked.

When telling a stranger what my job is ('professor of philosophical theology'), my first instinct, learned implicitly over years, is to check for the emotional response. This will set, at least initially, a sort of upper glass ceiling for how far the conversation might go, and how many further conversations there might be. This happens in microseconds, and at the level of bodily posture, and tension around eyes, mouth, shoulders, the scrunching of fists at the side of the body, a rapid blink. All of this is more important in the encounter than any explicit reasons or arguments that might ensue.

What we can attend to is the individual case and life story, oriented towards uncovering affect, emotion, memory, biography and feeling. Or, to put it more simply: we can attend to life.

*

Unearthing some of the work done by the concept of the divine, in the different contexts explored in the chapters of this book, does not, in itself, determine what judgements we might make about such uses.

This, in a way, is one of the claims of the book: that reason must reckon with a humility in the face of the concept of God, and that, consequently, there is a degree of non-coercive freedom when it comes to speaking about God, or not speaking about God.

At this point, I want to face head-on the 'variety = bollocks' instinct, which has surfaced a few times for us: that is, the claim that where there is such a wide variety of belief, it indicates that none of the beliefs are likely to be true.

In truth, I think there are a number of legitimate reactions to the variety of belief. I'll sketch three of them here, finishing with the approach that I associate myself with.

First of all, the determined atheist has a way to cope with the variety of types of belief in God. None of them are true. If this book has even partially succeeded, the atheist might concede that some uses of the God concept are not attempted explanations, and do not commit one to a belief in supernatural beings. They may, instead, evoke a certain type of attitude to the natural world: Stoic, say, or Spinozist.

But, the atheist may say, so what? With richer philosophical vocabularies, we can retain this conceptual space – acceptance, trimming our desires or fantasies of the life not lived – without the spookiness of divinity.

Also, a certain type of traditional theologian might agree with this atheist that yearnings for an unalienated life, for feeling at home in the universe, in themselves have nothing much to do with the God who reveals Godself in scripture, offering redemption from our fallen condition. Such a theologian might see the variety of types of belief, and insist, nonetheless, that only one type of belief, theirs, is true. Other explanations can be given for why so many people believe the wrong thing: sin, ignorance, chance, providence.

With the freedom and humility of reason in relation to the material presented, I cannot block either of these perspectives on the variety of belief.

However, I cannot accept either of them. I prefer to reach for an alternative approach. As I revealed in the last chapter, I have been formed in, and associate myself with, a strand of the Christian tradition. This tradition has, from within itself, committed theological grounds for being interested in, tolerant of, and patient in front of a variety of types of belief in God. I will not present, here, an argument *for* this committed theological position. In any case, an argument probably wouldn't work. I will show you the position as it moves in relation to the variety of belief. I will do this in the form of a thought experiment.

The experiment is simple enough: what might we expect if we combine a huge God – simple and omnipotent, omniscient, all-loving, and the creator of everything out of nothing – with our finite and limited capacities to know and apprehend such a God? Well, we might expect to receive the vastness of such a living God in fragments, shards, half-lights, both unveiling and distorting. And, if God is all-loving, we might hope that God can make God known to us in ways that are appropriate to our capacities, gifts and limitations.

The French Catholic philosopher Gabriel Marcel draws a distinction that can help us here, between a problem and a mystery.

A 'problem', Marcel writes, 'can be publicly formulated, using concepts that are "objective", and its solution can be discovered by anyone'. A problem requires hard work and research, until it is solved. A 'mystery', on the other hand, 'belongs to a realm of human experience that cannot be formulated publicly using objective categories, and its solution must be personal and individual.'[2]

Marcel considers that 'love, hope and faith' are mysteries and not problems. If the concept of God arises (or is resisted) in relation to a fundamental yearning to feel at home in the universe – to be free, to be significant, to be loved – then we are in the neighbourhood of love, hope and faith. The God concept is not a problem that can be solved. It is a mystery. And the proper attitude to mystery is humility, and the proper response, one made in freedom.

That we hit a limit to what reason and investigation can do in this area is not an accident. We have two types of reason for expecting to fail: some theological and some more broadly based on experience.[3] The theological grounds arise from the type of God that we speak of: simple, infinite, transcendent, eternal and outside of time (although about this, more in the next section of the book), yet equally present to each moment in time, the creator out of nothing. We should not expect to be able to fathom fully such an ineffable God. The more experiential grounds come to light when we think of all of the time spent arguing about God, over all the centuries, and the failure to arrive at agreement or certainty: all the disputation and disagreement, some of it peaceful and intellectual, some of it violent and primitive.

As I asked you to do early on in this book, think of your own case: how amenable are *you*, really, to a powerful argument or piece of evidence unsettling and changing your own belief or non-belief, or your long-held agnosticism?

So, when thinking and talking about God – that is, those of us who can't help ourselves, or stop ourselves doing this – what are we going to do next?

Well, to this, I say again: become attentive to the individual case and life story, oriented towards uncovering affect, emotion, memory, biography and feeling.

Or, to put it more simply: attend to life.

*

I can't write about your life, so, I'd better draw from my own. There is a rising interest in writing that draws from one's own life, or the biography of others: it is called 'life writing', and there are examples of it across the humanities, taking in politics, literature and philosophy.[4] Such writing, especially when reflecting on one's own experience, involves a balancing act between humility and a type of grandiosity, or self-indulgence. There is humility there, as one speaks from one's own experience, rather than imposing things on others, or saying how things must be for others. The danger of grandiosity or self-indulgence is clear also: why should others care how things are for you? In the end, the best check against this is the power and freedom enjoyed by the reader, simply to put the book down and walk away.

In the remaining three chapters, I am going to return to the opening vignette of the book: two men arguing at the top of a staircase. The older man, Richard Swinburne, was arguing that God should be conceived of as existing within time, if there is a God. The younger man, me, was arguing that God, if there is a God, should be conceived of as existing outside of time.

That such a debate was possible, indeed, that it was a required topic in a master's degree, in itself demonstrates something striking: that there exists a significant variety of types of belief in God, even within a single tradition, which in this case is Christian philosophical theology, drawing on Augustine and Aquinas, and Western philosophical treatments of the topic of time. Whether or not God is within or outside of time is a really significant difference of view, and both views are found in the same tradition.

What might be really going on when this disagreement comes to the surface?

I will suggest that it might be a different experience of the type of presence that we feel we need. I mean, in part, the presence of significant attachment figures, of whom parents are often our first and paradigmatic experience. I also mean the sort of presence that we have to ourselves at any moment in time: that is to say, what is my past self to my present self, and my present self to my future self? In what sense, and in what way, am I the same person over time? What is the unity, the chord, that makes a life *my life*, which, when it ends, is called 'a life'?

In all three of the remaining chapters, parenting and presence play a strong role. It is no accident that metaphors from parenting abound in religious traditions: God the father, of course, but there are also significant mothering images. In the book of Isaiah, for example, we read:

> Can a mother forget the baby at her breast and have
> no compassion on the child she has borne? Though
> she may forget, I [God] will not forget you!
>   … As a mother comforts her child, so will I
> [God] comfort you; and you will be comforted
> over Jerusalem. (Isa. 49:15, 66:13)

In the next chapter, I imagine what it might be like for Richard Swinburne to desire a particular type of divine presence, given some childhood experiences that he has generously put into the public domain. In the final two chapters, I offer experiences from my own life, of being a father, and of being fathered.

11

A Year in Bed

Why God might be in time.

I want now to return to the opening vignette of the book.

I described, in the autumn of 1996, two men arguing, in a room at the top of a staircase. One was Richard Swinburne, a significant philosopher of religion, the other, me, doing my master's degree.

They were disagreeing about what God would be like, if there is a God. Richard Swinburne was arguing that God, if there is a God, should be construed as existing within time, as you and I do, albeit with more powers and with no imperfections. I was presenting the position that God should be construed as existing outside of time, as being present, somehow, to all times, a bit like, say, numbers, or mathematical truths.

Although Richard Swinburne won the argument, as someone might win a chess game, I did not move my position at all.

I commented that neither, ever, change their mind, or persuade each other, and that they could meet once a week for a hundred years, and that nothing would ever change.

So, what was really going on, between these two men? Between Richard Swinburne and me?

In the terms that this book has been exploring, what might have been really underlying or motivating the abstract argumentative moves?

*

I feel that I know what was going on for me, and I'll tell you this in the next chapter. I cannot know in the case of Richard Swinburne, but I can imagine, or offer an interpretation. That is what I'm going to do in this chapter. First of all, I need to do a bit of setting up.

Richard Swinburne and I were having an argument within the Christian tradition. That is to say, we were assuming that God, if God exists, would have certain properties (which assumptions are shared also by Judaism and Islam): God would be all-powerful, all-knowing, perfectly good. Also, God would have a will, a freedom and an agency, and a capacity to love and reach out and be present to the creature, and to be in relationship with the creature. Of course, the way in which God has a will, enjoys freedom, and loves people is radically different from the way in which we do these things, as I've explored. But the point is this: whatever is valuable and significant about the way in which we love others, have a will, are free, and relate to others, *God enjoys these properties perfectly and fully.* The different way in which God loves others, is more, not less, than the way we love.

What I would like to emphasise here is the importance, within Christianity, that God is *present* to the believer, and in *relationship* with him or her: relationship is an interesting word, because it is not a fusion, or an utter remoteness, but an intimacy of two, intertwined, loving, involved. There is quite a contrast here with Stoicism or Spinozism: there, God is the word used for the nature of things, to which we must orient ourselves, bracingly and bravely. There is not a lot of love being sent to us from the Stoic Logos, or Spinoza's 'God or Nature'.

Think about the ways in which you need people to be *present* to you: partners, friends, lovers, parents, children. It is how we live, how we get by, how and why we are happy, when we are, and why and how we are sad, when there is absence, not presence, or not the right sort of presence.

Holding in mind the centrality of presence and relationship, within Christianity, we might look again at the four types of yearning that I've returned to throughout the book, as facets of the desire to feel at home in the universe. This time, I've added in italics a question under each about how this might receive a particular slant, when thinking about presence and relationship.

A yearning to address the problem of evil and suffering.

What sort of presence and relationship with us can help us to cope, and to hope for something better?

A yearning for significance, given the problem of the vastness of the universe.

What sort of presence and relationship with us will make us feel significant, and not so alone in the vastness?

A yearning for freedom, given the way in which we may feel determined by our genetics, or by vast historical and political forces.

What sort of presence and relationship with us will offer us a sense of freedom, a sense that we can breathe and move?

A yearning for a type of harmony and unity in our relationships with human beings and with non-human nature, given all the clashes and fractures in perspective that we encounter.

What sort of presence and relationship with us will promise a sense of harmony and unity with others, and with non-human nature, with all the clashes and fractures in perspective that we encounter?

With these questions about presence, and about relationship, in view, let's return to Richard Swinburne, and his conviction that God should be conceived of as being in time, if there is a God.

Remember, 'if there is a God' is still part of this. Anyone can play this game, atheist, believer or agnostic. I'm actually not really asking you what you think about God here, but more what you think about presence and relationship, in connection with our yearnings to be free, to be significant, to be at home, and not to be abandoned or alone in our suffering or distress.

*

To help us think about these things – presence, relationship, God and time – I'm going to draw on a remarkable long-form interview that Richard Swinburne gave as part of a British Library 'Oral Histories' project.[1] It is in the public domain, and anyone can read it, or even listen to the whole recording, which takes around nine hours. The interview ranges across Swinburne's entire life and career, from early childhood to future plans.

What I want to draw out here, though, is some of Swinburne's childhood recollections. When initially questioned, Swinburne seems a bit taken aback. Frequently, questions about early childhood are greeted with a rather astonished 'goodness', and a sharp intake of breath:

> My memories are not very good. Not because there's anything I sweep under the carpet, but because I don't think about the past very much, and if you

don't think about the past very much, you forget about it.[2]

As I think you might agree by the end of this chapter, his childhood memories are better than he initially thinks. Certainly, they are arresting, moving and winningly candid.

Before going into some of this material, I want to tell you a little more about Richard Swinburne's philosophical position, as it will help us to know what we are looking for in the childhood recollections.

*

I've commented a few times on Richard Swinburne being a towering intellectual figure in philosophy of religion.[3]

Why is he that?

It is not particularly because of the concept of God that he puts forward: all-powerful, perfectly good, perfectly free, all-knowing. These are the properties that have traditionally been ascribed by Christians to God. For our purposes, there are two ways in which Swinburne is distinctive. The first is the one I've already mentioned several times: that Swinburne conceives of God as existing in time. He is not alone in this. I'd say the academic field of theologians and philosophers of religion is pretty evenly divided on this, although the view that God is outside of time is the more traditional pre-modern view, shared by Augustine and

Aquinas, for example. That doesn't mean, necessarily, that it is right, of course.

The second distinctive feature of Swinburne's thought is what I'm going to name, for reasons that will become clear, 'the gathering of fragments and scraps'. This is my description, not his. Swinburne thinks not in terms of dogmatic certainties, but in terms of probabilities. Swinburne draws on understandings of probability that are used by many scientists. These approaches are called 'Bayesian'. Bayesian probability is a framework that scientists use to weigh up the plausibility of alternative hypotheses.

The weighing up of alternative hypotheses can become quite technical, as a lot of Swinburne's work is. But, for our purposes, we only need to know a few things.

Swinburne believes that the existence of God is more likely than not, and more likely than other possible explanations of why the universe exists as it does, and of why we have certain religious and moral experiences and intuitions. He is willing to piece together incrementally small probabilities, until they amount to something that we can do something with. So, for example, Swinburne allows the probability of God existing to mount up, as we consider a range of things, such as religious experience, our sense of morality, our sensitivity to beauty, and historical testimony about miracles. Each of these in themselves might be too fragmentary to base belief in God on, but taken together, the scraps add up to something.

Given the properties that God has – perfectly good, all-powerful and all-knowing – Swinburne considers that we can work out that it is more probable than not that God would act in certain ways: for example, with regard to how God would deal with the suffering caused by our sin and imperfection. In turn, we have a significant range of duties in relation to God, given all that we owe to God.

A lot of philosophers like Swinburne's work. He is highly esteemed. But, at the same time, as with anyone who does anything interesting, he is also a figure of some controversy. When people don't like Swinburne's thought, it is often the weighing up of probabilities that comes under attack. Two sorts of concern tend to arise. First of all, that there is not enough respect for the mystery and otherness of God: of what it is to believe in God, and who and what God might be, and what God might do. There is an anxiety about Swinburne trying to work out all his probabilities. There is too much confidence in our ability to judge probabilities in the face of mystery and unknowing. How can we possibly know what is 'probable' that God might or might not do? Language about God is used quite directly, without much sense that God is radically different to human beings: God is simply a more powerful and better version of what we are. These are one set of concerns.

There is then a second set of concerns about a lack of commitment, both positively, when believing in God, but also negatively, when dealing with doubts or despair: we do not declare, in church, or in joy, that we 'believe that it is more likely than not that you, oh God, exist'. Some theologians prefer to talk of rapture, on the one hand, and then the darkness of the soul, the despair of doubt on the other: saying God's existence is 'more probable than not' can seem a bit vanilla, lacking soul and passion.

These two sets of concerns can be summarised like so: too much about human reason (probabilities), not enough about passion.

I'll return to these criticisms later in the chapter. Part of my claim will be that humanising Swinburne's philosophy, by appreciating some of his life experiences, helps to counter some of these critical concerns, or to soften them, and to change their aspect somewhat.

So, with these two features of Swinburne's thought in view – God being in time, and fragments and scraps – let's hear from him about some of his earliest religious formation. It will take a few pages for the relevance of the material to become visible.

Let it unfurl a little.

*

About his childhood, Swinburne reflects, 'I cannot remember a time when I did not believe that there was a God. And that applies to five, six as well as much later.'[4]

His parents, he remembers, were not particularly religious. Swinburne admits that he has no idea when, or how, or from whom belief in God came. But the belief was there, emerging with self-consciousness, and it never faltered.

This, I can identify with, having come out, as I've already mentioned, religious.

We see that the question, 'God or Nature', or 'God or not God', was not one that received critical enquiry, the weighting of arguments and evidence. It is a given, going back into childhood like breath itself.

Swinburne reports being 'much more closely connected to my mother', than to a rather absent father, who 'was very involved in his musical activities'. The marriage, he comments a few times, 'was not a happy one'. A memory he does provide of his father is when, at the age of 'seven, eight, nine, that sort of thing', he 'played the organ in a Congregational Church':

> I remember him taking me to sit in the organ loft,
> which I found very exciting, lots and lots of pipes
> and so on that small children could get under, but
> big people couldn't.

'Most of the things I did', Swinburne writes, 'I did with my mother': 'yes, she used to take me on picnics', 'we were pretty poor, it was wartime and so there weren't many places to go to and we didn't have much money to go there'.[5]

At around the 'age of ten', Swinburne recalls being 'diagnosed with possible TB', and 'as a result of that I spent most of the next year in bed'. Disarmingly, Swinburne recalls:

> I think I sort of got used to being in bed, so I wasn't very anxious to get up again.

Perhaps unnecessarily, but, winningly nonetheless, Swinburne explains:

> I did [get out of bed] eventually.

Swinburne continues that 'because my mother obviously wanted me to, because she thought that would be best for me', he went to 'boarding school'. When he went back home in the holidays, Swinburne 'knew nobody and just read my books and did my scrapbooks and so on':

> I was pretty lonely as a child at that stage.[6]

The interview then moves on to later memories, and Swinburne's education. But, then, there is an interesting caesura in the flow of conversation. The interview is picked up the next day, and Swinburne asks to return to some of the earlier memories, almost, as it were, to put the record straight, to do justice to his mother, and to recount something quite intimate and precious, to get something off his chest. Swinburne begins the next day by saying, 'Yes':

> Although all the answers I gave to you were correct, I felt that I hadn't put what happened into perspective, partly because although I'm aged eighty, I very seldom think about my past and I'm always looking forward, even at the age of eighty, to what I'll be doing next year, and that sort of thing. So I hardly ever think about my past and it was only being interviewed by you that forced me to do so, and therefore to think that I hadn't brought out certain things about the past.[7]

What Swinburne wants to emphasise is his debt to his mother, and his loneliness, and what the presence of God meant to him in connection with both. Swinburne recalls his solitariness from the time of 'being ill for a year'. Swinburne then corrects himself, revealing that he did not have the suspected TB after all. In another disarming moment, he offers an alternative description to 'being ill for a year', 'or at any rate in bed for a year'.

The holidays were 'a very lonely time':

> I came home of course in the holidays, but I, being an only child – I was an only child, I had no friends then because they all went to other schools and they

hadn't seen me for a year anyway when I was away in bed, so I was entirely on my own.

His mother was 'out every weekday from morning till evening at work earning money to pay for my schooling'. Although home 'some of the time', his father did not interact with the young boy: 'he kept very much to himself in his own room, in his study':

> I was on my own for these long school holidays… and sure, I read books and went for walks and listened to the radio, but it was a very solitary time and no doubt that's had a great influence on the rest of my life when I feel I have also been relatively a fairly solitary person.

This solitariness 'in general' was 'the situation and no doubt it's influenced me a lot subsequently'. At this stage in the interview, there is something of a breakdown in the usually smooth and pristine prose in which Swinburne speaks, with grammatically incomplete fragments of speech:

> Secondly, I didn't bring out, perhaps I did, but I'd like to repeat, my religion.
>
> I was very conscious from ever since I can remember that although I was on my own in these respects, God was my companion and I kept this

hidden largely from my parents for some years, almost waiting till they'd said goodnight to me and then saying my prayers when they wouldn't see me.

And that was the dominant theme of my – dominated my solitariness.

Following this, Swinburne also wants to 'say one thing about my mother'.[8] Again, the language is somewhat broken:

I think she – I obviously owe an enormous amount to her, she put everything into me, her own marriage was unhappy, [one sentence deleted at interviewee's request] and she and he were living in the same house but didn't often see each other really very much, and we certainly never did things together as a family in any way after I went to school, away to boarding school. It was a very hard life for her and she had no friends really and she put everything she got into me and that of course in due course I found rather oppressive. But nevertheless, it was because of that that she had these various ambitions for me and that clearly encouraged me to think highly of myself and to think that I could do things. And obviously I must be grateful to her for that. Those are the things that I think I meant to say. Clearly there were exceptions to all of these things, but basically that I remember very strongly.[9]

This is a delicate thing to write about. Swinburne has generously offered what we might call intimate psychic material, and one wants to handle this with tact and sensitivity, and with due humility about knowing what it might signify for his wider work. What follows then is not to be misunderstood: I am reporting what the material *makes me think of in relation to Swinburne's system.* This is not an attempt to access the deep and personal intentions or motivations of Swinburne. I have no access to this at all. It is a speculative and possible interpretation, a self-conscious, sheer and explicit projection, based on a significant, but relatively thin, data set: the long-form interview.

I've said Richard Swinburne was my doctoral supervisor – and an excellent one at that. I am exploring the way in which understanding something about Richard Swinburne's experience opened up for me, positively, a feature of his philosophical system that I used to regard with something approaching a sort of cold contempt.

With this important caveat in place, we might consider the solitary boy, alone hour after hour, in bed for a year, and then further alone in the holidays, his father away or inaccessible, his mother sacrificing herself for his schooling, and the schooling compounding his solitariness. The adult recalls God being his constant and only companion during these times. What sort of figure might companion such a boy? What sort of figure could provide *presence* and *relationship*, in response to various yearnings? What sort of presence, inside or outside of time, might help a boy not to suffer from loneliness, but to endure it? What sort of relationship might help a boy to be significant in the vastness, even when alone, and to be in harmony with others, even when the others are absent, and to hold different perspectives in peace together, even when the perspectives are being pulled apart?

The presence offered by the God companion might mirror and resemble the missed and absent mother, and exhibit a sort of domestic reliability, an industrious care for the boy and the world, working hard, and being dutiful, without any romantic *Sturm und Drang* which would upset the boy's equilibrium. The possibility of using some sort of direct and non-mysterious language in relation to this God figure might be important. And, now, a striking feature of Swinburne's philosophy of religion may come into sight for us: that God is *in time*. The boy feels the solitary passing of time, hour by hour – 'entirely on my own' – and any companion who can offer solace and presence must be similarly in time, hour by hour, accompanying the boy. The companionship offered by this God figure gives the boy a confidence in being alone, in being solitary. Swinburne reflects about subsequent solitariness that, given his childhood, 'I have been able to cope with this quite easily'. This can also be seen at work in Swinburne's independence of mind, project and purpose: his lack of concern with being fashionable, and his determination to swim upstream intellectually.

What about the other feature of Swinburne's thought, the fragments and scraps, the weighing of probabilities, and the lack of either certainty or despair?

Swinburne recalls 'an incident in 1940' when living in Tiptree, a village in the English county of Essex:

> I remember being in the garden of the house, it had a long garden there, and my mother was hanging out the washing and seeing all the sky was covered with German aeroplanes flying on their way to bomb London, and I remember saying to my mother, 'Gosh, surely God wouldn't let the Germans win.' And I remember her giving me a rather ambiguous answer: it seemed to me at the time an ambiguous answer.[10]

As I've commented, Swinburne's appeal to Bayesian probability theory is often critiqued, or comes under suspicion, for not being committed and passionate enough, for 'hedging its bets', if you like. But there is another way of looking at it: Bayesian probability is indeed all about a lack of knowledge and certainty. But this is not the same as a lack of deep commitment and yearning. It is all about how to weave a web that holds one, and enables further enquiry and life, even with all the gaps and absences. There is an engagement with something like mystery, with unknowing, with our small and vulnerable minds, in the spinning of Bayesian webs. The boy, doing his scrapbooks and taking his walks, weaves as well as he can a blanket of security, even with partial threads and material: the father in the study, the mother at work, the ambiguous answer about the German planes. He gets in and behind the pipes of the organ, finding shelter where a 'big person' would fail to fit.

*

What are we to make of all this? What does it add to the more formal understanding and appreciation of a philosophical system? In my own case, I feel it gives a great deal. From my undergraduate days, Swinburne has loomed large in my academic life. Alongside a personal respect for him, which grew as I was exposed to his sense of duty and intellect as a doctoral student, I could never warm to the religious sensibility of his philosophical system. It seemed cold and presumptuous, ascribing likely intentions and properties to God. But reading the interview transformed all of this. The directness of the relationship to God, a companion in loneliness, and the placing of God in time, became something quite moving, vivid and living, once we can feel the breeze of the potential mineshafts deep into memory and childhood. It is the living and breathing faith of a vulnerable and rational creature. His argument became humanised for me.

Does this make the approach, which focuses on affect, 'reductive', concerned no longer with truth or falsehood, but with a type of psychological usefulness or fit?

No, I don't think so.

Staring at the sun will blind us. Just so, the Biblical tradition tells us that to experience God directly is unbearable for human beings. 'You cannot see my face, for no one may see me and live' (Exodus 33:20), God tells Moses. Taken theologically, if God is real, comprehending and containing all of reality, with depths beyond that which we can fathom or tolerate, why would God not appear to each of us in the form that is just about bearable, stretching us only so far, as we grow into ourselves? God is a companion. Why would God not first and foremost appear in this way to the boy, and this be conserved, refined and made intellectually powerful in the man? Who is to judge, at the most intimate level, our inner life with God, if and where we are happy to talk in these terms? Theology knows that differences in the reception of God have more to do with differences in our capacities and formation. God is a large enough reality to accommodate all this.

Who knows what someone else carries through life? Who can know, and who can judge, what is carried from childhood solitariness, or the witnessed suffering of a self-sacrificing mother, or the deleted sentence about the parents' unhappy marriage?

12

Is It Over?

Why God might be outside of time.

Conceiving of God as existing outside of time might seem to make God remote, uninvolved, far away.

That's not how it has felt to me.

Perhaps it all depends on how one feels about time: do you feel at home in it? Or, can it seem, sometimes, like a sort of trap, a prison, a problem? How does time, and being in time, relate to the fundamental types of yearning that I have identified: for relief from suffering, for freedom, for significance, and for a harmony of perspectives?

How you feel about time, and yourself in time, and at different times, may impact the type of presence and relationship you hope for, with God, if you believe in God, and with yourself, if you believe in yourself.

Something crystallised for me during the 2020 Covid-19 lockdown, about God and timelessness, and it seemed to me that I was able to identify 'what was really going on' when I defend a conception of a timeless God, and was able to understand, really, why I had been so drawn to Kant's philosophy, where space and time are not fundamental to reality.

I'd like to tell you about the experience, and the realisation that followed. It begins with kicking a ball about.

*

In 2020, I would go walking with our then nine-year-old son, Rory, for exercise, and for (not much of) a change of scene. Or, we might kick a ball around on the 'bowling club' lawn – a shared communal space in the West End of Newcastle-upon-Tyne.

Visible on the walk, or from the bowling club, was a half-built 'high-rise' block of flats. The plan was for 'Hadrian's Tower' to reach twenty-seven storeys. This is not much for many cities, but for Newcastle, a relatively low-rise area, it was *tall*.

Local opinion was divided. But we were excited about the building – Rory and I – calling it a 'skyscraper', and admiring the artist's impressions of the sleek green and black glass, and, most of all, the promised restaurant and bar on the top floor. I imagined prosecco so chilled that the glass was misty with condensation. Rory shared his vision of a hot chocolate piled with marshmallows and thick swirled cream.

Construction was halted for a bit, because of the pandemic, until they had worked out protocols and regulations for Covid-safe working, and, a few months later – maybe more, I forget – the construction began again. The recommencement of the build was a sign of hope for us. The skeletal shape began growing again. We watched and counted the floors being added: thirteen, fourteen, now sixteen? How had we missed fifteen? Had they done two at once?

There was something that we liked to do, in relation to the building as it grew. Early on in the pandemic, when things were particularly scary – 'what was going to happen?' – we did it every day. As we settled into more of a pandemic routine, we did it less often, maybe once a week, or every fortnight.

'Wave to our future selves,' I would say.

We would then wave, sometimes furiously and jokingly, sometimes a bit poignantly, aiming our gaze at where we estimated the top floor of the tower would eventually be.

This was on my instigation. At first Rory humoured me, and then seemed to like it, and would sometimes spontaneously issue the instruction himself, which I would immediately obey. He never questioned the practice. I guess, at nine years old, so much of what grown-ups make you do seems pretty arbitrary, and without much immediate profit.

We imagined ourselves inside the swanky new restaurant – Rory called it 'fancy'. We were twenty-seven storeys in the air, standing by the glass wall, looking out over the bowling club, or along the whole length of the downhill road that leads into the city centre. We – our future selves – were waving with magisterial kindness and comprehension, and without any sense of embarrassment, at our past selves, us, now, waving at our future selves. Our future selves were out and about, in a post-pandemic world, sharing anecdotes about the hard days – the (now) hilarious 'maths' 'lesson' that ended in us all shouting at each other, with coffee splashed, inexplicably, all the way down the staircase, like the murder scene of a coffee-based life form, even though nothing had been thrown or dropped. Or, we would recall the day the new puppy chewed the router, meaning that we were without Wi-Fi, which meant without the breath of life itself. How funny it all was really, and how good to think that we had survived it, the three of us, together, stronger in the end – really, we should say the four of us, including the new puppy, Ciara, whose future self would be an adult Labrador.

It gave us, me anyway, huge heart to imagine our future selves thinking of us now, cheering us along, 'don't give up', 'you'll come out the other side'. We don't know that *now*, of course, but *they* do, our future selves, and they are thinking about us, pulling us through.

Our future selves have a modest crowd of waving past selves to greet and encourage: our past selves in the middle of the bowling club lawn from 15 May 2020, and then a similar pair to the left of this, my hair longer and more unkempt, from 20 June 2020, and near-identical groups from most days in between. There would be a throng of us walking down Westgate Hill towards the tower, coming into the town centre, all looking up and waving. More of us yet – past selves – on the other side of the tower, visible from different streets, which we had also walked along. The future selves might almost feel like royalty. Everyone below seems happy to see us. It seems to mean a great deal to them that we are here.

When this thought about the numerous past selves occurred to me, me the 'past self' of 2020, I had mixed feelings about it. I sort of wanted a more intimate quaternal moment with the future selves – those two then waving just at us two now. I wondered how I would feel about it, in the future, when looking down at us all. Would I be able to love us all equally?

In retrospect, I now realise that I was sharing with Rory one of my habitual spiritual practices, going right back into my own childhood, which has tendrils going into many core aspects of my adult intellectual sympathies and scholarly endeavours.

I know I am not the only person to have had the thought that the meaning of any particular event is largely determined by the future. Kierkegaard said that life has to be lived forwards, but can only be understood backwards.[1] Just so. The meaning of an event, within a life, is determined by how it sits in a narrative. Like a note in a musical score, it may sound dissonant and ugly, or beautiful and soulful, depending on what comes next. The salience of this moment now is held over, with the capacity to be transformed and reconfigured, and only revealed later, with the possibility of further transformations. The past is not over, and the future can change the past. The past is constantly being reshaped and re-envisaged.

In this moment, March 2020, the first Covid lockdown is just beginning. Is this the beginning of the end? Will the social fabric hold? Will zombie-like citizens be smashing shopfronts and burning cars? Will I die? Will you? Later on in the lockdown, the question changes, maybe. Will you kill me? Or I you?

Or, is this now a time of resilience that we get through together, coming out stronger, and more grateful for ordinary life? The present is pregnant with possible futures, and we have no certainty which will be delivered.

That is to say, we do not know what is *here now already*, waiting to be born.

We do not know what is happening right now, or what has just happened, until the future rises up to meet us.

Pandemics, wars and terrible illnesses provide dramatic examples, but there are smaller and more quotidian examples all the time.

What does it mean that I did not answer honestly the delicate question put to me today?

What does this argument, this rift, this distance, this atmosphere, mean? Is it the ending, or an unhealable wound? Or the beginning of sometime truer and more fitting?

Is this swelling in the neck a nothing, a sore throat, a product of my imagination, or, is it the first day of a dark adventure with some hideous cancer?

One of the scouring and abysmal things about betrayals, secrets and rifts is that the future can raid the past, ripping up scrapbooks, shredding photo albums and smashing souvenirs. These future things can sneak into and enter the past, even where they had no existence or presence at all, at the time. Time-past seems to be something that can be intruded upon as easily as someone returning to the same place. It can be vandalised just as easily as a revered old building.

I cannot know, here and now, how things will unfurl, and how the future will shape the past. But my future self does know, and understands.

At points in my life, when things are difficult, and it is not easy to see a way through, I imagine my future self praying for me, willing me through with a sort of ardour and determination. And I know that *this* at least will happen, whatever comes of it – unless, of course, I die, and, even then – because, generally when things are easier, I *do* pray for my past self, usually with a particular focus on a specific dilemma or sadness. This is, I suppose, the sort of deal I must make: if I imagine my future self waving at me now, or praying for me, I need to make sure I really do it, when that future comes. Then I know that I can trust myself in the future to do this, because I have done it in the past, praying for other futures, which have now already occurred. I've done this for as long as I can recall, before going to sleep, since being a boy, doing my private prayers, in relation to all sorts of difficulties: a miserable period of feeling persecuted at school, say, or during the frightening illness of a loved one, or during a period of torpor, or of obligations that feel impossible, because I can neither meet nor avoid them.

So, I envisage a future self praying for a past self, where the past self is aware of this happening in the future. The prayer is addressed to God, where God is conceived of as outside of time, and not trapped within it, as I am. This does not mean, for me, that God is remote from time, or distant from it. The point of eternal timelessness is that God is equally present to and intimate with every time, and is able to be equally present to my future and past selves. The prayer of the future self has a pathway into the 'gone' past, which is not gone to God. The point is, time can feel like a trap: this atmosphere, this chaos, this unhappy place, this painful process, this mourning, this grief, this hell, this dilemma, this obsession. God is free of time, and in speaking to God, I share somewhat in this freedom.

Those selves are in the sight and love of God, just as real as this embattled and partially blinded self here and now. Swinburne, he says, does not think much about the past, but focuses on the present and future, with God as his constant companion. I think too much, perhaps, about the past and the future. I hardly know what it is to 'live in the present', except that it sometimes overwhelms, and except to contemplate how the future shapes the past by passing through this vanishing geometrical point. God is also my constant companion, present to my whole life, freeing me from the partiality and limitations of the fragments of just this present slice of it. God's timelessness brings me closer to my whole self, promising some sort of integration. Some psychoanalysts tell us that the two great existential threats that we are thrown into at the moment of our birth are abandonment and being overwhelmed.[2] God, in God's mercy, does not abandon Richard Swinburne, and God, in God's mercy, does not permit me to be overwhelmed.

None of this is at all rigorous. It is 'to think feelingly, to feel thoughtfully',[3] responding to a pull, a draw. I have read rigorous defences, and critiques, of the coherence of divine timelessness. We are back now to the opening vignette of this paper: a student and his supervisor disagreeing using formal arguments. In the M.Phil. supervision, I was attempting to defend the account of divine timelessness offered by Eleanore Stump and Norman Kretzmann.[4] Swinburne was arguing for his own position, where God is in time.

In this vignette, we have a vivid study in the limits of a certain type of argument and rationality.

There we were, in 1996, two men arguing.

Or, were we, really, two boys, stubbornly protecting what we needed, what we had always needed – and, maybe, what God had given us – to get through it all?

Watching these two figures now, I see the pair of us arguing on the sand, with our backs to the wide wild ocean.

What, in any case, is 'time', and what do we know about it, such that we can discuss or determine whether something is within it, or not?

I'm put in mind here of Judith Wolfe's description of the work done by theology:

> Yes, theology constructs. It constructs metaphysical accounts of the world; it constructs theories and images to guide us. But they are light, tentative, humble, because when we construct theologically, we are not building towers; we are building boats. And we trust the sea.[5]

In any case, my draw to divine timelessness, such as I understand it, is an experience, laden with affect and emotion, and with memory and expectation.

My first vivid 'experience' of it was, in fact, when surrounded by the sea, on the Isle of Iona, when visiting on a retreat at the age of sixteen. I had a sense that I would visit Iona many times, and that in some sense, each visit was as one time – a hub, with corridors leading out to all my selves, at 16, 20, 24, 36, 50, until…well, the numbers run out. Iona, is, of course, a physical and geographical space, which can be revisited. Somehow this symbolised, for me, the way in which God, a conceptual and theological space, who is always there and can be revisited, contains a whole life.

As I've mentioned, up until 2020, I spent nearly fifteen years dedicated to reading, interpreting and writing about Kant.[6] I articulated an interpretation of Kant that construes our 'proper selves' as existing alongside God – somehow – beyond space and time, where space and time are, for Kant, the forms by which we receive the real world, including our true selves. I did this because I am convinced this is the correct interpretation of Kant, of his so-called 'transcendental idealism', and because I find it fascinating, and surprisingly coherent, given Kant's deeper and wider assumptions. But, in terms of the 'what is really going on?' question, there might be more to say: that I 'get it', or get something of what someone might be protecting by construing God, and themselves, as timeless. Time, for some, can feel like a trap, isolating, splitting, disintegrating. God is freedom. When I am with God, outside of time, when I am 'on Iona', I partake in freedom. I am not trapped forever in this moment, in this chaos, isolation, solitude or unhappiness. There is a yearning for freedom, and for significance in the vastness, and for a harmony of perspectives, of different parts of my life.

*

In the summer of 2022, Rory and I did go to the restaurant/bar at the top of the newly completed tower. It was good. We walked around the room, which occupied the entire top floor, and waved regally down on all our former selves. We may have looked odd. Certainly, we giggled a little. I was initially glad to see that Rory was not embarrassed, although, now nearly twelve, he was plenty old enough to find me embarrassing, even when I'm behaving 'normally'.

Of course I then worried that, perhaps, he had not been sufficiently socialised, because of lockdowns, to progress to the essential life-stage of feeling embarrassed by parents.

In any case, I felt that the exorbitant price of the (compulsory-for-entrance) 'afternoon tea' – dry cake, under-seasoned sandwiches – meant that we could claim a little latitude.

We are in no rush to go again. Rory said that the hot chocolate was not the best, either.

I don't really know where to direct my 'waves to my future self' now.

I've also recently become concerned that my future self only ever prays for *me*.

This seems selfish. I wonder if I should ask him to pray for others. But they might not want that. As a spiritual practice, it might seem too messed up: people might not want any part in it. I've decided, on balance, that I should pray for the past selves of others, wishing joy and healing where it is wanted.

So, who knows when, or where, I might brush past the ghost of my future self, thinking of me now, or of others, if it can rise to the challenge of being less self-absorbed?

And with this whimsical practice, grounded on an implausible (but not impossible) thought, there is, for me, something divine in the air. That is how I feel about it.

I can't help myself.

All of this, and more, is evoked, promised, stirred up – for me – by the 'doctrine' of divine timelessness. There is no point in trying to dissuade me – either of the doctrine or the practice.

I won't listen.

But I will listen, avid and alert, to why you think otherwise. *That* is very interesting to me.

13

After Life

When God is absent.

My late father, Jim, died unexpectedly on the last day of 2016.

On 1 January 2017, I found, much to my surprise, that I had lost my faith.

It wasn't that I had encountered an argument, or some sort of intellectual problem with it: 'I can't believe that God would take my father', or something like that.

Before, in relation to faith, I had always known, I thought, that I certainly wasn't following my father. I was doing it all by myself, with God's help.

Doing it all by myself?

The idea of the freedom of belief had been an important one to me, as it is for many others. For Thomas Aquinas and others in this tradition, we do not have evidence for faith that compels assent, in the way that you simply have to accept that $1 + 1 = 2$.

Rather, the evidence for faith does not compel: faith is not impossible or contradictory, but, also, it is not compelling. That is where freedom comes in. The will has to choose to accept with a type of commitment, which amounts to a different type of certainty, and the believer asks God's help with this act of the will.

This way of understanding things meant a lot to me. It seemed to combine a humility about what we know, and a depth of commitment, which satisfied deep needs in the human spirit.

So, I was willing my faith, doing it, as I thought, 'all by myself', with God's help.

Dad was somewhere else, doing his stuff – I might say, 'his crazy shit', because his faith had always seemed quite different from mine.

What was really going on? And what had the faith, and its felt absence, to do with the different types of yearning: in relation to suffering, freedom, significance and a harmony of perspectives?

To explore all this, I'll need to say something about Dad and his faith, and how it seemed so different from mine, and, yet, why mine turned out to be more dependent on it than I had realised.

*

Almost the only thing, in his whole life, that my father did quietly and unobtrusively, was leave it. Silently, upstairs, at home, he stepped through the door from which there is no return.

In other ways, though, his death did have some of his characteristic features. He certainly surprised us. And there was a symbolic panache in leaving on the last day of the year. Dad loved to find patterns, symbols, meaning, in numbers and dates, as in all things.

I remember contemplating, with Dad, in the 1990s, an exhibition of Picasso's artwork. Dad's favourites were a series of drawings, where Picasso had tried, with a single line of unbroken charcoal, to capture the spirit and the essence of a living reality. If I were to attempt such a line about his life, I would say that Dad strived life-long to join in, and to spread, God's own delight, God's own smile at creation. And to love God, Dad was convinced, means loving many things. Dad was a great lover of things: from Herodotus to celandine flowers, and from T. S. Eliot to tea-cakes. His rather ordinary second-hand Peugeot car, Dad was convinced, obviously resembled a delicate oriental pagoda on wheels. On a rainy Welsh day, Dad would marvel at the sheen and sparkle of the light and the dark on some roof slates, finding an apposite line from Isaiah to capture their drizzly splendour.

*

My late father was a devout Roman Catholic, who had a deep devotion to Our Lady, but also had an affection for and draw towards Hinduism. He was around in the first two years of my life, which, of course I don't remember. I met him for the first time, consciously, when I was sixteen years old, and we built a strong relationship. He imbibed in me the beauty and living spirituality of the more Platonic and poetic strands of the tradition, with its saturation in symbol, music and liturgy. He had a powerful and expansive intellect, and a fertile and surprising imagination. Everyone agreed with this – even his detractors.

Just to say this much is a bit rose-tinted, because there were some less comfortable feelings in the neighbourhood also. There were aspects of Dad's faith that I found, frankly, superstitious, almost pre-modern, and pre-Enlightenment.

He would receive words from God at communion: actual instructions and information.

Once, God even told him to drink more:

Drink deep, Jim, drink deep.

God had said that, apparently.

This was the sort of divine feedback his friends and family could do without. In the last year of his life, Dad insisted someone else finish off the bottle of wine at dinner:

I've had about five times more wine over my life-time than I ought to have done – this will help even things out a tiny bit.

Only five? I thought, but didn't say.

He would pray to St Anthony if he needed to find something that was lost. He was convinced that the prayer was causally effective. He would touch a rosary hung from the rear-view car mirror, and ask for divine help, to find a parking place.

Are we doing spells here, I would wonder? Okay for witches, but Catholics?

He would talk to wasps, asking them to leave the room.

'It really works,' he would insist, nodding furiously, in the maddening way he did, when saying something palpably ridiculous.

He was irked by measures to restrict the use of wine at communion on health grounds – enacted during the bird flu scare of 2006. Dad was convinced that consecrated wine *would not* and *could not* pass on infection, because it had been consecrated, and had become the blood of Christ: as if this gave it some sort of antiseptic properties.

Too absurd.

And, then, there was his passion, which could be anything from embarrassing to wild. I remember him angrily heckling a priest in the morning Mass. He profoundly disagreed with the homily. Or, he might weep whilst singing a particular hymn. Once, he even cried about Agincourt, for heaven's sake – out of pity for the French. He loved France.

He could be too many for me. Too much.

He was an artist. If anyone asked him what he did, his job – 'what do you do?' – he would say, 'I'm an artist.' He was,

I think, a good artist, but if a job involves money, it wasn't a job. Whenever anyone liked one of his pieces, he would just give it to them.

He drew Blake-like religious pictures, covered in calligraphy, sometimes Latin, sometimes Greek or Hebrew. He did a degree in theology in his sixties, and won Lampeter University's prize for studies in Hebrew. He would draw swirling saints, swans, boats, sacred hearts, roses, seals, mixed, incongruously, with a London bus, maybe. Or, he would make large ceramic 'sun-bursts': huge plates covered in religious symbolism and narratives, the raising of Lazarus, maybe, next to sheaves of wheat. He made chunky ceramic rosaries, as large as fishing nets, and would pray with them for hours a day, endlessly smoking his pipe, and downing small buckets of strong coffee.

In contrast to Dad, I felt that my faith was more refined, more intellectual, more modern, more modest and cautious, more elegant, urbane, compact, contained, more nuanced.

My faith was less unhinged.

I thought, really, that it was, in some ways, probably most ways, 'better'.

*

After he died, though, it became clear that there was only a path there, because he was not far in front of me, pushing through, gently marking a trail, as can happen in a densely ferned forest.

He had been, all the time, just ahead of me, shrouded by cloud and mist. He had hidden himself to give me the encouraging impression that I was doing it for myself.

I had no energy, no willpower for faith, no libido for it.

It was just torpor and ashes, and fallen pride.

It wasn't that there was an intellectual problem, a new 'argument': 'I can't believe that God has decided to take my 76-year-old, diabetic, deep-drinking, determined pipe chain-smoking father', or something like that. It was an emotional and spiritual problem – a lack of spirit. I didn't even have the energy to become an atheist or agnostic. I just didn't care.

I had had no idea what he had meant to me, or, what his batshit faith had been doing for me, all that time.

I was lost in the woods, and felt myself inside the perspective of the son, walking this time in front of his father, on the way to school, in Cecil Day-Lewis's poem 'Walking Away':

> With the pathos of a half-fledged thing set free
> Into a wilderness, the gait of one
> Who finds no path where the path should be.

*

I began the book talking about the different types of yearning, to which God can be a type of answer.

> A yearning for a type of harmony and unity in our relationships with human beings and with non-human nature, given all the clashes and fractures in perspective that we encounter.

I quoted Judith Wolfe's account of the Christian hope that all the perspectives upon our lives might come together:

> [T]heology believes that we are not the ultimate tellers of the stories of our lives; that our lives are, indeed, part of a larger story, in which we do not have to be perfect protagonists, but are, as sinners loved by God, forgiven and restored to a story in which love places *all* at the centre and *all* at the service of others.[1]

Perhaps like many children mourning parents, one of the things I found was a loss of self, as well as the loss of a parent. You lose *that way* of being known and seen in the world, unique and distinctive to the parent's gaze and way of loving and knowing you.

A dad wants his boy out there, busy and happy in the world, stretching out, unfurling, being fully himself, as long as he is kind, and as long as he is safe. That wanting had gone from the world, and its absence was quietly and undramatically appalling. All the hours left to live, without a father to want you to be alive, in the way that only you can be, without the paternal seal:

How good that you are.

My mind goes back again to the poet and essayist, Jeremy Hooker, also quoted in chapter 2.

Hooker, we recall, suggested that the word 'God' might stand for a 'need that makes an idea possible', which is 'the need to think that, though we cannot fully know ourselves, there is a perspective in which we are fully known'.[2] Hooker brings to light the fragments that make up our lives, where 'complete self-knowledge and complete knowledge of another person are equal impossibilities':

> With our mixed motives, with the knot of contradictions that we are, and with the relationships that make us, as beings subject to change, who live in time, there is no position from which we can gain complete self-knowledge. We are always on the inside of our own faces, and in life, so that ideas of the self tend to be waxwork ideas, perceptions of ourselves as effigies.[3]

Jeremy Hooker – Jerry – was my father's closest and life-long friend.

Hearing Jerry speak of Jim, and Jim of Jerry, their story is one of talking, talking, talking: on beaches by firelight in their teenage years and twenties, Jim playing the mandolin and singing, Jerry reading his poems. Both looking over the Solent:

> [A]mazed to think of France,
> So far away, still serving wine.

These lines are taken from Jerry's poem 'Friend with a Mandolin'.[4] Dad is the friend with a mandolin.

As I said before, Dad loved France.

Then they talk on long walks in the New Forest, or in the Welsh mountains, or hitchhiking penniless across the continent of Europe, or, when rescuing each other at times of crisis, chaos and breakdown. Winding forward several decades, they are still talking, now on phones from their hospital beds, both diabetic, and in my dad's case, hit by a car coming out of church, a 'lucky' amputee/survivor, and in Jerry's case, surviving a stroke. In the end, both in wheelchairs, re-married, happy, grateful, gracious, and as rebellious, bold, vital, boisterous, tender and non-conforming as they had ever been.

And now, as I write this, Jerry widowed, still thinking and writing every day, sometimes talking with me on the phone, and Dad, dead.

Their lifelong conversations, it occurs to me now, embody somewhat one of the questions of the book: 'God or Nature'.

Jerry is an established and esteemed poet, academic and literary scholar, who self-identifies variously as a sceptic, an agnostic, an animist, or as a (bit of a) pantheist, drawn to a literary paganism and romanticism, with a feminist anger about the pernicious patriarchy of Christianity, both in its symbolism and in its institutions. Certainly, he reveres nature, and is sometimes called a 'nature poet'. Jim, Dad, had great gifts, but he did not 'establish himself', and was, according to his own self-description in his seventies, a man with 'a great future behind him'.

The last full day I spent with Dad was in October 2016. I remember him on the sofa, at home in South Wales. Rosemary, his wife since 2003, knew how to operate the remote control to get the desired channel, and had given Dad accurate advice. Dad found out, in due course – quite a lot later – in his own way.

> 'Why didn't you just do what I told you?' Rosemary asked.
>
> 'Rosemary,' Dad replied, rubbing the stump of his amputated leg, and adjusting his spectacles, which were repaired with Sellotape, 'I didn't get to where I am today by doing what people told me to.'

This was followed by his low, bronchial, pipe-smoked laugh, and eyes creased with a type of merry self-knowledge.

*

When thinking about Jerry, I have in my mind's eye a photograph of Dad and Jerry, leaning on a gate, squinting into the camera.

But, I realise, the photograph is an impossible one: it depicts Jerry as he is now, in his eighties, and Dad in his mid-fifties. But they are (were) the same age.

I realise that the photograph I have in mind is actually of me and Dad: me about seventeen, Dad around fifty-one, about my age now. In the actual photo, I have disastrous orange hair: I had tried, too many times, to return my then-brown hair to its boyhood ash-blond.

In my mind, I had switched Jerry for me.

The confusion about the photograph gives me a sort of comfort, somehow. One of the sadnesses I felt, when I lost the energy for faith, was a sort of guilty distance from Dad: our shared faith was important to both of us. Feeling that I had lost it increased the distance between us, as did each day of being in a world without him wanting me alive.

I had let him down. Abandoned our shared space. I hadn't wanted to, or chosen to, but I had.

But, then, I thought of Jerry.

Dad loved Jerry, and would not change anything about him, as far as I could see. Jerry seemed to feel the same about Jim, Dad. They did not try to convert or persuade each other, or, at least, they knew that such an exercise would be futile, but talk and talk, and talk, about God, or not God, they did. And it helped them, and sustained them, and helped them to grow in empathy and compassion, for each other, and for others.

God or Nature.

Jim or Jerry.

If Dad could love Jerry, and not mind the difference in faith, he could love me still, and not mind. He could love this way of me being in the world.

A father to a son, as I said above, wants his boy out there, busy and happy in the world, stretching out, unfurling, being fully himself, as long as he is safe, and as long as he is kind.

It felt as if something had been restored. A way of being seen: by Dad somehow, and through the eyes of Dad's closest friend, who has become a confidant, friend and correspondent to me.

Jerry recently sent me this poem, set in a landscape on the south coast of England, near where I, Jerry and my parents, grew up. It is a salty, silty, muddy, grassy coastal area, called the Salterns, with a melancholy, minor-key beauty. It is the location where the photograph I have just spoken of was taken.

The 'friend', the 'Catholic friend', who appears towards the end of the poem is my father, Dad:

Salterns

1
A cloud of steam filled
the boiling house;
salt impregnated the air;
roads all around were
black with coal ashes
from the furnaces
incessantly burning.

2
Below the seawall,
when the tide was out,
we dug in the mud for ragworm.
Behind the wall, a memory
of water diverted into tidal trenches,
solutions of brine, and an industry
that produced riches for some
by preserving fish, meat and vegetables,
and worked others to death.

3
In old times, the salterns ran
from Lymington to Hurst spit.

I loved them best at Pennington Marshes,
when I was walking with my friend
and a salt wind off the water
was blowing fresh air into our faces.
It was somewhere that I always expected
the otherworldly to reveal itself.
My Catholic friend suspected idolatry.
'There's no special place,' he cautioned.
 'Every place is special, because God is everywhere.'
I have not forgotten, and when I return
to the Salterns now, in memory,
I think of his words
and my dead friend walks with me.

Just so. As with place, so with time. 'Every time is special, because God is at all times', and because of this, paradoxically, I return in memory to those special times, and special places, thinking of 'his words'.

Again, all of this, and more, is evoked, promised, stirred up – for me – by the 'doctrine' of divine timelessness.

*

We've already encountered, in chapter 5, the atheist claim that belief in God arises as a defence-mechanism against mortality and death.

I've come to think, in my own case, that these atheists are onto something, but not for the reasons they give: death does have a lot to do with belief in God, but not because of some fantasy about the continuation of life after biological death.

I literally don't care about that, or have any sort of view on it. How would I know? How could I?

It is more at the level of feeling, metaphor, pain, love.

It is because death is a limit, which reveals the nature of love. Death is the ultimate and final limit, but we are preparing throughout life for death, with other limits and boundaries.

Judith Wolfe reflects on Thomas Aquinas' definition of love:

> To love is to wish for the good of the beloved and
> to wish to be with them.[5]

Wolfe draws attention to the 'characteristic of love', that it 'places us in situations where we have to choose the wish for the good over the wish for union':

> [W]hen our children leave home, or when we have
> to let go of someone for their own good.
>   But this is only because in pursuing our desire for
> union otherwise than by choosing to prioritize the

beloved's good, we would pursue it in such a way as to destroy its object: there is, in fact, ultimately no way of being with someone we love healthily except by willing the good for them, because the person will no longer be themselves. And the very *pathos* of our choice for the good of those we love, when it means letting them go, arises from a contrasting wish for closeness, which is present even, and perhaps especially poignantly, in its renunciation.[6]

*

In the opening to this chapter, I said that Dad was a great lover of things, because to love God, Dad knew, was to love many things.

Dad spent hours and days in the final years of his life 'tidying his study': the 'study' being a tiny smoke-stained box-room, with self-installed make-shift shelves that you might expect to find in a greenhouse or garage holding nails, hammers and screws. Instead, these shelves bent precariously under the weight of Herodotus, Dante, books with images of the greatest stained-glass windows, the Jerusalem Bible. I could never understand why it took him so long to tidy such a tiny space: years, it seemed, never with any evident improvement in the situation. When, after his death, I went through his papers, notes, letters from friends (so many), books, I could see the problem. Rather like a metaphor for his life, his liver and his lungs, he had tried to stuff at least five times too much – more like fifteen times too much – into a finite space. Just as he could never really tidy up himself, the study could never be tidied. It was, in principle, impossible. If you moved one thing, something else had to be moved, because nothing could be thrown away. It was like a claustrophobic smoky kaleidoscope. You could shake it, and the pieces would change their pattern, but there was always the same amount of stuff.

The box-room was a symbol for Dad's raids on life: he had loved, sought the good and union with, perhaps too many things, people, disciplines, thoughts, possible futures, now impossible pasts. He had come up against too many limits, and then reacted by making further forays, adding more limits, until he met the final one. A few years before his death, Dad had made the remarkable choice to stop smoking. Pipe-smoking, along with praying, socialism, and drinking, was, I had always thought, one of the immoveable pillars of his faith. He did it so that he might live to see Rory become sixteen, the same age I was when I first made contact again with Dad, after a childhood mostly apart.

Poignantly, on the desk, was a freshly bought and used bag of pipe tobacco, with his pipe on its side, the tar-blackened pipe cleaners stuffed into a used coffee cup. I didn't mind. I was glad he had enjoyed a pipe in the last few days. I hoped that he had enjoyed it.

As I looked at the dead pipe, I remembered a scene from around ten years before. Dad was making his third pot of strong tea, having drunk two pots in about an hour. He paused, looking slightly surprised by his excess, and said:

> Boyle had a law.
> Insole's law, it seems, is: if something is worth doing
> at all, it is worth doing a great deal too much of it.

*

As I went through all of Dad's papers, I found a Biblical passage written out by him, again and again: sometimes in beautiful calligraphy, sometimes written hastily on the back of an envelope in biro. It comes from the 'Song of Solomon':

> Set me as a seal upon thine heart, as a seal upon thine arm:
>   for love is strong as death; jealousy is cruel as the grave:
>   the coals thereof are coals of fire, which hath a most vehement flame. (Song of Solomon 8:6)

That 'love is strong as death' is something that one feels, when it presses against the strength that death is. It is commonplace now to hear complaints that we do not talk enough about death. I've also heard a lot about death being 'natural', and not something to be afraid of. But there are other options, between being afraid, and accepting something as natural. There can also be a sort of disbelief that accompanies the acknowledgement of the inevitable.

Karl Jaspers, the twentieth-century philosopher, speaks to this:

> We can know death in general and yet at the same time there is something within us which instinctively regards it as not necessary and not possible.[7]

In the nineteenth century, the philosopher Schopenhauer reflected:

> It might be asked how much each man in his heart actually believes in a thing which he cannot really conceive; or whether perhaps…our own death does not seem to us at bottom the most fantastic thing in the world.[8]

Behind such half-disbelief may be a sort of protest. As the philosopher Maritain puts it, death is:

> [N]ot so much frightening as incomprehensible…a violation, an insult, an offense.[9]

Christian theology can regard death through a double aspect. From one perspective, yes, death is natural. As the Catholic theologian Karl Rahner puts it:

> Death is the most universal thing, and every man declares it is natural and a matter of course that one dies.

But, then, completing the quote, Rahner puts forward the other perspective, the force of which I admit to feeling:

> And yet there is alive in every man a secret protest…[10]

Even when we accept death, do we not weep? And it is love that makes us protest.

Gabriel Marcel puts this point powerfully:

> To love a being is to say, 'Thou, thou shalt not die!'[11]

The Catholic philosopher Josef Pieper comments on this line:

> And what is imparted to the lover faced with the actual death of the beloved person who 'must not' die is that he himself experiences this death – for in this case, it is not really 'another' who is dying

– not just from outside, but as if from within. He is accorded an experience which comes as close as humanly possible to the dying person's experience of his own death.

The word 'lover' should not be misunderstood in romantic terms, as if we were speaking of… passionate love as the prerequisite of this kind of experience… Rather, we are speaking of that wholly selfless affirmation which can be read in the eyes as they gaze upon the beloved, an affirmation which says: How good that you *are*!

… No one experiences the pain and dreadfulness of death and dying so thoroughly as one who loves.[12]

*

I know, I know, that not everybody feels the same about death. I might think of the Stoic, discussed in chapter 5, or the humanist, in chapter 3. I am mindful of the variety of feeling and thinking here. I want to understand you, when you tell me how it is different for you, not so as to overcome you, or persuade you, but to love you a little bit more, or like you, anyway, if love or liking is what you want. I want, in any case, better to understand what is good for you, and how to be with you, even if only in a conversation. At the very least, we might clarify why we can't get along.

But this is how it is for me. I began the book saying that I came out religious. When I'm taken out feet first, that will be how it is also.

It seems I have kept faith with faith after all, although now it exists in a different form. Perhaps it all feels a little sadder, less exultant, more adult, and yet more...well, unhinged.

In any case, I no longer sense that I'm doing it all by myself, with God's help. It's not by myself at all, not really, although I trust it is with God's help.

Earlier, I said that my first thought about why I believed in God was:

I believe in God because of the problem of evil.

This has changed. Now, I believe in God because of death, and what it reveals about love, the love that remains after life.

*

It's not much of an argument, is it?

Well, I did warn you.

But, it has at least two things in common with arguments.

First of all, it probably won't make you change your mind, one way or another.

And also, this: in an argument, we come up against limits, of what we can know, or affirm, or deny, or devote ourselves to, and of whom we can persuade, and of what. In this way, an argument mirrors the wider life of which it is a part, with all its limitations – what and whom we cannot help but love or forsake – up until the final limit.

When the argument reaches its limit, something else might arise from the silence: weeping, looking, a sheepish smile, acknowledgement and, perhaps, a different way of talking.

*

In August 2017, seven months after Dad died, Jerry sent me another poem: 'At a Requiem Mass: *In memory of Jim Insole*'.[13]

Jerry wrote:

> It isn't adequate – how could it be? – but it is the best I'm capable of.

I replied, 'it isn't adequate, it is beautiful', or so I found it:

> With the words of the priests,
> with their movements,
> in front of the coffin,
> under the holy images,
> I find myself,

now here, now there,
walking with you, treading
again in the steps of a lifetime.
…
Anyone who desires faith
will receive it, you said.
Forgive me –
as you always did –
this splinter of unbelief.
The way I have taken
is uncertain as a cliff path,
or a track disappearing,
where the trees close in.
…
When you played and sang
there was magic
in common things.
It was an enchanted world
you played and sang into being.
I think of the mandolin
with no one to cradle it,
coffined in its box.
We are the singers today
and you the silent one.
…
It was not another world
you lived in, but this one

as it truly is, constantly renewed
by the Bread and Wine.

…

What is the world unless
the world that's given
in friendship and love.

…

Light where imagination
fails, perpetual,
without shadow,
where I envisage you
walking away, vanishing
in eternal welcome
So I hope, restless
with spoken words
that draw me back to the sound of our steps
scrunching dead leaves
or shingle at the sea's edge.

…

For you, God
was everywhere.
If everywhere, then here – where the river surges,
turbid and brown with autumn rain,
acorns falling
around us as we walk
further in, talking and talking.

…

A green woodpecker crosses a glade.
Silence falls
after the echo of its laughing call.
the only sound is distant voices,
where we have disappeared among the trees.

Acknowledgements

A few friends and colleagues read earlier drafts of this book. I am deeply grateful for the time and care they put into this, and for the invaluable advice and feedback so generously offered. Special thanks to Anna Beer, Mat Bevis, Andrew Chilton, Ben DeSpain, David Dwan, Lexi Eikelboom, Ed Epsen, Karl French, Joshua Furnal, Sam Jordison, Karen Kilby, Simon Oliver, Judith Wolfe and Annabel Yeo.

In supporting me to find the time and space to think about and write this book, I am indebted to two projects funded by the Templeton Religion Trust, both of them parts of the overarching project 'Widening Horizons in Philosophical Theology'. My own project explored the limits of a certain conception of reason in relation to belief in God. A group of theologians, philosophers and literary scholars, atheists and believers and somewhere in between, met and enjoyed honest conversations. The participants, whom I thank, were Akeel Bilgrami, Clare Carlisle, Ben DeSpain, David Dwan, Lexi Eikelboom, Philip Goff, Jennifer Herdt, Karen Kilby, Simon Oliver and Mark Wynn. Another project to which I am indebted, run by Clare Carlisle and Karen Kilby, explored the possibility of different ways of writing about philosophy and religion.

My thanks to the department of theology and religion at Durham University. I have been honing and teaching some of the material in this book for many years, and have been constantly enriched and encouraged by conversations with colleagues and students.

For their enthusiasm, encouragement and wise advice, I am grateful to Novin Doostdar and Rida Vaquas from Oneworld Publications.

For conversations about the book, and for sharing and shaping the experiences that go into the work, I give special thanks, of course, to Lisa and Rory. And, for shaping this wider life, I am forever grateful to Linda, Mike, Sue, Lucie, Joan and Alec, and many others too numerous to list.

This book is dedicated to my father, James Insole, and to his friend, Jeremy Hooker: to Jim and Jerry.

Whilst the manuscript of this book was going through its final proof-reading stage, on 26th December 2025, at the age of 84, Jerry died at home, with his son Joe by his side. Jerry had read and approved the manuscript and was happy with my intention to dedicate it to him and to my father. Jerry was the dearest of friends to my father, and he became a true friend to me also. I'll always remember him and be grateful (in so many ways) for his life, humour and wisdom, which was lightly worn, but warm. I hold Jerry's children – Joe and Emily – in my thoughts as they join me, with so many others, on the foothills where those who mourn their fathers gather.

Notes

Chapter 2

1 William James, 'The Varieties of Religious Experience: A Study in Human Nature', in *William James: Writings 1902–1910* (New York: Library of America, 1987).

2 Ibid., 436.

3 Blaise Pascal, *Pascal's Pensées* (New York: E.P. Dutton & Co., 1958), trans. by William Finlayson Trotter, fragment 425, p. 113.

4 St Augustine, *Confessions of St Augustine* (New York: Sheed and Ward, 1959), trans. by F.J. Sheed, 1,1.5, p. 113.

5 Thomas Nagel, 'The Absurd', in *Mortal Questions* (Cambridge: Cambridge University Press, 2012), 11–23, 15.

6 Ibid.

7 Jeremy Hooker, *Diary of a Stroke* (London: Shearsman Books, 2016), 163.

8 Ibid.

9 Judith Wolfe, *The Theological Imagination: Perception and Interpretation in Life, Art, and Faith* (Cambridge: Cambridge University Press, 2024), 39.

10 Ibid., 40.

11 Ibid., 40–1.

12 Ibid., 41.

Chapter 3

1 Matthew Engelke, '"Good without God": *Happiness and pleasure among the humanists*', in *Values of Happiness: Towards an Anthropology of Purpose in Life*, ed. by Iza Kavedžija and Harry Walker (London: Hau Books, 2017), 133–61, 134.

2   Ibid.

3   Ibid., 133.

4   Ibid., 134.

5   Ibid., 140.

6   Ibid., 137.

7   Ibid., 142.

8   Ibid.

9   For all these details I am, of course, drawing directly on Engelke, "'Good without God'", 136.

10   Matthew Engelke, 'The Coffin Question: Death and Materiality in Humanist Funerals', *Material Religion* 11(1), 26–49, 32.

11   Ibid.

12   Richard Dawkins, *The Magic of Reality: How We Know What's Really True* (Bantam Press, 2011), 31–2.

13   Ibid., 21.

14   Ibid., 198.

15   Ibid., 97.

16   All the Einstein quotes are taken from Max Jammer, *Einstein and Religion* (Princeton, New Jersey: Princeton University Press, 1999), 48, 49, 52, 67–8, 73.

17   John McDowell, *Mind and World* (Cambridge, Mass.: Harvard University Press, 1996), 109.

18   Ibid., 85.

19   Thomas Nagel, 'Evolutionary Naturalism and the Fear of Religion', in *The Last Word* (New York and Oxford: Oxford University Press, 1997), 127–43, 130.

20   Ibid.

21   See, for example, Brett Mercier, Stephanie R. Kramer, Azim F. Shariff, 'Belief in God: Why People Believe, and Why They Don't', *Current Directions in Psychological Science* (2018) 27/4, https://doi.org/10.1177/0963721418754491.

22   See Nathan Heflick, 'Five Causes of Belief in God: Things that Cause Belief in God May Surprise You', in *Psychology Today*, 26

February 2012, https://www.psychologytoday.com/gb/blog/
the-big-questions/201202/five-causes-belief-in-god.

23 Bernard Williams, 'Philosophy as a Humanistic Discipline', in
Philosophy as a Humanistic Discipline 180–99, 181.

24 James, *Varieties*, 436.

25 Edwin Muir, from 'The Incarnate One'.

26 https://www.wsj.com/articles/BL-SEB-56643, accessed
26/08/25.

Chapter 4

1   This reported exchange with a journalist may be apocryphal. The
first mention of it is reported in the *Seattle Times*, years after
Gandhi's death in 1948. See the *Seattle Times*, 23 January 1967,
'Ad Paid Off For Swedish Beauty' by C. J. Skreen, Quote Page 6,
Column 7, Seattle, Washington. (GenealogyBank).

2   See Akeel Bilgrami, *Secularism, Identity, and Enchantment*
(Cambridge, Mass., and London: Harvard University Press,
2014), especially chs. 4–6.

3   Paul Tillich, from 'The Depth of Existence', in *The Shaking of the
Foundations*.

Chapter 5

1   John Sellars, *Lessons in Stoicism: What Ancient Philosophers Teach
Us about How to Live* (London: Penguin Books, 2019), 66.

2   Dawkins, *The Magic of Reality*, 31–2.

3   Ibid.,177–8.

4   Marcus Aurelius, *Meditations* (London: Penguin Classics, 2006),
Bk 10, 18, p. 99.

5   Ibid., Bk 9, 40, p. 91.

6   Pierre Hadot, *The Inner Citadel: The Meditations of Marcus
Aurelius*, trans. by Michael Chase (Cambridge, Mass.: Harvard
University Press, 2001), 75–6.

7   Epictetus, *Discourses*, IV, 7, 6, cited by Pierre Hadot, in *The Inner Citadel*, 95.

8   Hadot, *The Inner Citadel*, 95.

9   Pierre Hadot, *What is Ancient Philosophy?* (Cambridge, Mass.: Harvard University Press, 2004), 95.

10 Ibid., 156.

11 *Stoicorum Veterum Fragmenta*, I, 179.

12 Pierre Hadot, *What is Ancient Philosophy?*, 138.

13 Epictetus, *Discourses,* IV, I, 100–1. Cited by Hadot, *The Inner Citadel*, 96.

14 Aurelius, *Meditations*, Bk 2.17, p. 15.

15 Ibid.

16 Ibid., Bk 9.32, p. 90.

17 Sellars, *Lessons in Stoicism*, 33.

18 Sellars, *Lessons in Stoicism*, 66.

Chapter 6

1   For a meditation on the power of the 'imagined otherwise', framed through a discussion of George Eliot's *Middlemarch*, see Clare Carlisle, *The Marriage Question: George Eliot's Double Life* (London: Allen Lane, 2023), Ch. 9.

2   Jammer, *Einstein and Religion*, 49.

3   Spinoza, *Spinoza: Ethics Demonstrated in Geometrical Order*, ed. by Matthew J. Kisner, trans. by Michael Silverthorne and Matthew J. Kisner (Cambridge: Cambridge University Press, 2018), preface to Part 4, p. 158.

4   For a more atheist Spinoza, see Stephen Nadler, *Think Least of Death: Spinoza on How to Live and How to Die* (Princeton: Princeton University Press, 2020). For a panentheist reading of Spinoza, see Clare Carlisle, *Spinoza's Religion* (Princeton and Oxford: Princeton University Press, 2021).

5   Rebecca Newberger Goldstein, 'Explanatory Completeness and
    Spinoza's Monism', in *Spinoza on Monism*, ed. by Philip Goff
    (London: Palgrave Macmillan, 2013), 281–90, 285.
6   Ibid.
7   Ibid., 284–5.
8   Ibid., 284–5.
9   Ibid., 284.
10 Spinoza, *Ethics*, in *The Collected Works of Spinoza,* ed. and trans.
    by Edwin Curley (Princeton: Princeton University Press, 1985),
    Part 1, Proposition 11, 417; cited by Goldstein, 'Explanatory
    Completeness', 285.
11 Goldstein, 'Explanatory Completeness', 285.
12 Ibid.
13 Ibid., 285.
14 Ibid.
15 Ibid.
16 Ibid.
17 Ibid.
18 Ibid., 288.
19 Ibid.
20 Ibid.
21 Ibid., 290.
22 Ibid.
23 Ibid.
24 Ibid.
25 Ibid., 288.
26 Jammer, *Einstein and Religion*, 49.

Chapter 7

1   Iris Murdoch, *The Sovereignty of Good* (London and New York:
    Routledge, 1989), 80.

2   Influential 'metaphysical' readers of Kant include Karl Ameriks, Rae Langton, Desmond Hogan and Andrew Chignell. More deflationary commentators include figures such as Henry Allison and Andrews Reath. A previous generation of commentators, represented by Peter Strawson, tended to read Kant as having metaphysical commitments, but in a way that was thoroughly disreputable and contrary to the deepest principles of his thought.

3   Commentators who read Kant as attempting, but often failing, to express a philosophical Lutheranism, combining elements of Platonic theological rationalism, include Palmquist, Pasternack, Wood, Kain, Marina and Kanterian.

4   References to Kant refer to the *Akademie* edition, *Kants gesammelte Schriften*, edited by the Royal Prussian (later German) Academy of Sciences (Berlin: Georg Reimer, later Walter de Gruyter & Co., 1900). These references are cited by 'volume: page number', and are prefaced by an abbreviation of the title of the work, as set out below.

   CPrR   Critique of Practical Reason in *Immanuel Kant: Practical Philosophy* (Cambridge: Cambridge University Press, 2008), trans. and ed. by Mary J. Gregor, 5: 3–309.

   GW   *Groundwork of the Metaphysics of Morals,* in *Practical Philosophy*, 4: 385–463.

5   For this analogy, I am indebted to the work of Merold Westphal, 'In Defense of the Thing in Itself', *Kant-Studien* 59 (1968), 118–41.

6   Murdoch, *The Sovereignty of Good*, 80.

7   Elizabeth Bishop, 'On Being Alone', in *Poems, Prose, and Letters*, eds. Robert Giroux and Lloyd Schwartz (New York: The Library of America, 2008), 323.

Chapter 8

1   Christopher J. Insole, 'Autonomy, Value and the Unalienated Life: An Interview with Akeel Bilgrami', in *Redeeming Autonomy:*

Theology, Agency, Social Justice, eds. Christopher J. Insole and Benjamin R. DeSpain (London and New York: T&T Clark, 2025), pp. 163–76.

2   Bilgrami, 'Gandhi (and Marx)', in *Secularism, Identity, and Enchantment* (Cambridge, Mass.: Harvard University Press, 2014), 122–74, 157–8.

3   Akeel Bilgrami, 'Value and Alienation: a Revisionist Essay on Our Political Ideals', in *Nature and Value*, ed. by Akeel Bilgrami (New York: Columbia University Press, 2020), 68–88, 70.

4   Ibid., 74.

5   Ibid., 71.

6   Insole, 'Autonomy, Value and the Unalienated Life: an Interview with Akeel Bilgrami', p. 170.

7   Bilgrami, 'Value and Alienation: a Revisionist Essay on Our Political Ideals', p. 71.

Chapter 9

1   For this example, I am indebted to Janet Martin Soskice, *Metaphor and Religious Language* (Oxford: Oxford University Press, 1985), 131.

2   Soskice, *Metaphor and Religious Language*, 140.

3   A. J. Ayer, *Language, Truth and Logic* (Harmondsworth: Penguin Books, 1971), 156. Cited by Soskice, *Metaphor and Religious Language*, 144.

4   Cited in 'Introduction', *Anselm of Canterbury: the Major Works*, eds. Brian Davies and G. R. Evans (Oxford: Oxford University Press, 1998), pp. vii–xxiii, viii.

5   Anselm, *Proslogion* in *Anselm of Canterbury: the Major Works*, pp. 82–104, 1, pp. 84–5.

6   Anselm, *Proslogion*, 2, p. 87.

7   Ibid., 26, p. 103.

8   Ibid., 26, p. 104.

9   Ibid., 25, p. 101.

10   Ibid.

11   Ibid., 25, p. 102.

Chapter 10

1   'Into the Feel Tank: Remembering Lauren Berlant and
     Her Concept of "Cruel Optimism"', https://lithub.com/
     into-the-feel-tank-remembering-lauren-berlant-and-her-con-
     cept-of-cruel-optimism/, accessed 18 April 2023.

2   This is quoted from Clare Mac Cumhaill and Rachael Wiseman,
     *Metaphysical Animals: How Four Women Brought Philosophy
     Back to Life* (London: Penguin, 2023), 136. For this account of
     Marcel, I am indebted to this work. Mac Cumhaill and Wiseman
     acknowledge a debt to Brendan Sweetman, 'Introduction', *A
     Gabriel Marcel Reader* (South Bend, Indiana: St Augustine's Press,
     2011), 5.

3   For this insightful distinction, I am indebted to the D.Phil. thesis
     of Joel Gutteridge, 'Philosophical Theology and the Limits of
     Explanation', presented at the University of Oxford in January 2024.

4   For an example of this genre in philosophical theology, see
     the work of Clare Carlisle: *Philosopher of the Heart: the Restless
     Life of Søren Kierkegaard* (London and New York: Allen Lane,
     2019), *The Marriage Question: George Eliot's Double Life*, and
     Transcendence for Beginners (London: Fitzcarraldo Editions,
     2025), Carlisle draws respectively on the lives of Kierkegaard,
     George Eliot and her own experiences.

Chapter 11

1   'Richard Swinburne Interviewed by Paul Merchant', British
     Library Oral Histories: https://sounds.bl.uk/sounds/richard-swin-
     burne-interviewed-by-paul-merchant-1001306757940x000002.

2 Ibid., 2.
3 Richard Swinburne has numerous publications, but the core of his position is set out in his trilogy: *The Coherence of Theism* (Oxford: Clarendon, 1977), *The Existence of God* (Oxford: Clarendon, 1979), and *Faith and Reason* (Oxford: Clarendon, 1981).
4 Ibid., 5.
5 Ibid.
6 Ibid., 3.
7 Ibid., 24.
8 Ibid.
9 Ibid., 24–5.
10 Ibid., 5.

Chapter 12

1 For a philosophical – Kierkegaardian – life of Kierkegaard that meditates on this insight, see Clare Carlisle, *Philosopher of the Heart: The Restless Life of Søren Kierkegaard* (London: Allen Lane, 2019).
2 For this thought, I am indebted to James Hollis, *Hauntings: Dispelling the Ghosts Who Run Our Lives* (Asheville, North Carolina: Chiron Publications, 2013), 47.
3 See Clare Carlisle, *The Marriage Question: George Eliot's Double Life* (London: Allen Lane, 2023), 266. This is in the context of discussing the marriage of thought and feeling in the work of George Eliot.
4 Eleonore Stump and Norman Kretzmann, 'Eternity', *Journal of Philosophy* (1981), 78: 429–58.
5 Judith Wolfe, *The Theological Imagination*, 26.
6 Christopher J. Insole, *Kant and the Divine: from Contemplation to the Moral Law* (Oxford: Oxford University Press, 2020), *The Intolerable God: Kant's Theological Journey* (Grand Rapids: Eerdmans, 2015), and *Kant and the Creation of Freedom: a*

Theological Problem (Oxford: Oxford University Press, 2013). For articles, see the following: 'Free Belief: the Medieval Heritage in Kant's Moral Faith', *Journal of the History of Philosophy* 57.3, 501–28; 'Kant, Divinity, and Autonomy', *Studies in Christian Ethics* 32.4 (2019), 470–84; 'Kant on Christianity, Religion, and Politics: Three Hopes, Three Limits', *Studies in Christian Ethics* 29.1 (2016), pp. 14–33; 'A Thomistic Reading of Kant's *Groundwork of the Metaphysics of Morals:* Searching for the Unconditioned', *Modern Theology* 31.2 (2015), 284–311; 'Kant's Transcendental Idealism and Newton's Divine Sensorium', *Journal of the History of Ideas* 72.3 (2011), 413–36; and 'Intellectualism, Relational Properties and the Divine Mind in Kant's Pre-Critical Philosophy', *Kantian Review* 16.3 (2011), 399–428.

Chapter 13

1 Wolfe, *The Theological Imagination*, 40–1.

2 Hooker, *Diary of a Stroke*, 163.

3 Ibid.

4 Jeremy Hooker, 'Friend with a Mandolin', from the 'Solent Shore' collection, republished in *The Cut of the Light: Poems 1965–2005* (London: Enitharmon Press, 2006), 78.

5 Judith Wolfe, '*Who by Fire?* Love at the Limit of Being', keynote plenary paper at the British Society for the Philosophy of Religion (unpublished), 2023, p. 5. Wolfe cites Eleanor Stump as drawing upon this account of love, which is paraphrased here. The paper will be published in a forthcoming volume, *Love, Religion and God,* ed. by Fiona Ellis and David Worsley (London and New York: Routledge, forthcoming).

6 Ibid., p. 7.

7 Karl Jaspers, *Psychologie der Weltanschauungen*, 231. All the passages on this page are cited by Josef Pieper, *Death and Immortality* (South Bend, Indiana, University of Notre Dame Press, 2000), trans. by Richard and Clara Winston, 48–50.

8   Arthur Schopenhauer, *Sämtliche Werke*, vol. 2, 1270.

9   Jacques Maritain, *Von Bergson zu Thomas* (Cambridge, Mass., 1945), 146.

10   Karl Rahner, *Zur Theologie des Todes*, 49.

11   Gabriel Marcel, *The Mystery of Being*, vol. II, *Faith and Reality* (Chicago, 1960), 171.

12   Pieper, *Death and Immortality*, 12–13.

13   Published in Jeremy Hooker, *Word and Stone* (Bristol: Shearsman Books, 2019), 79–83.

About the Author

Christopher Insole is Professor of Philosophical Theology and Ethics at the University of Durham. He is the author of *Negative Natural Theology* as well as two major works on Kant's thought: *Kant and the Divine* and *The Intolerable God*.